DATE DUE

P9-APE-077

black and (A)broad:

traveling beyond

the limitations of identity

First edition September 2010

First Published Netherlands 2010 by adelaar books

ISBN 978-94-90906-01-6

Printed by Lightning Source

Front Cover image by Emmalene Stockton

Book Design by Creationbooth.com

With all my love,
I dedicate this memoir
to my mother,
Beverly Jenkins Vines

Seated, left to right: Cory, Dawn, me, Felicia

Standing: Mom and Dad

Toledo, Ohio ca. 1971

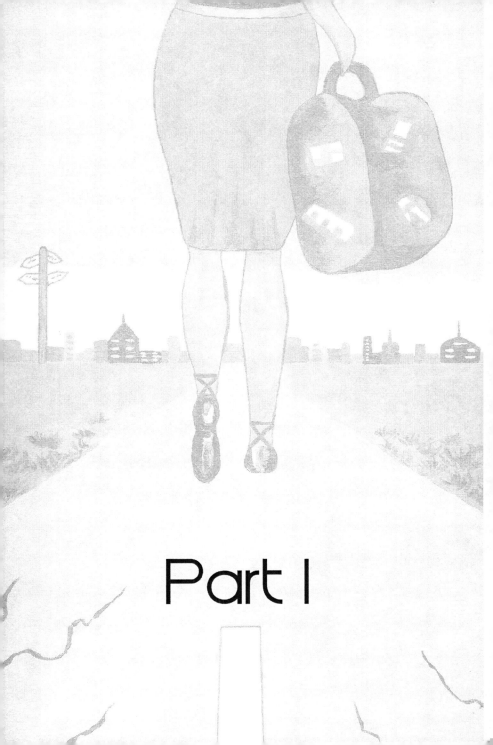

Part 1

"Child, who's going to do your hair if you take off with this man to Holland?" challenged a voice inside my head not even a minute after my Dutch boyfriend of two years asked me to move back "home" with him. And rightly so because Holland wasn't exactly known as the Mecca for black hair care. It wasn't like when I'd moved to Washington, D.C. (a.k.a. Chocolate City), where I could get my hair done on every other street corner.

"Girrl, you'd best be asking him if there are any black people over there," needled the voice before I could find an answer to the first question. *"Now, you don't want to get over there and have those people ready to lynch you."*

I knew Vinz was waiting for an answer, but I couldn't stop my eyes from darting around the den of our rented duplex in New Orleans, where we'd been living together for the past year. My gaze stood still on the computer I'd charged to my MasterCard and was still trying to pay off. Instead of meeting Vinz's blue eyes, I focused on the built-in bookshelf filled with the books I'd collected as a graduate student of Latin American literature. Each title glared back at me as if to say – in Spanish no less:

"You are a strong, independent black woman who has supported herself all of her adult life without the help of any man. Are you gonna let this man, this … this … foreigner, who doesn't know Jack about what it's like to be a black woman in America, take away everything you've worked so hard to get? Doesn't he know that black American women don't have the option of throwing caution to the wind, packing up and running away to an exotic country – with a white man no less? Doesn't he know that black people need other black people around? Doesn't he know that not everybody can do a black woman's hair? Obviously not, otherwise he wouldn't be asking you to give up everything you know."

Yes, he wanted to go home to *his* family, to *his* friends, to *his* culture. What about me? I had packed up my life the year before to move with him to New Orleans, and now he was asking me to do it all over again. Did it not occur to him that I'd have to leave behind the friendships I'd spent decades cultivating, family that had known me for a lifetime and a culture that had defined me? Looking past him into our sparsely-furnished den, it hit me right then and there that, without him, I couldn't afford to pay the rent we'd been sharing. Without him, I didn't have any ties to this city that I had discovered with him and that I had grown to scorn because of its disturbing racialized environment. Where else would I go if I didn't go with him?

The initial shock of receiving that fateful invitation from the love of my life was slowly turning into anger for putting me in this vulnerable position.

Still, I was silent.

The ticking from the big round clock with the silver finish that we'd bought together months before was the only sound in the den. I could have sworn those ticks were speaking to me:

"Carolyn, you're not married to this man. What's gonna happen if you get into an argument with him? You know his friends and family are gonna side with him. Who's gonna get your back? Monika and Michelle, your girls since second grade, are gonna be on another continent. With a six-hour time difference, you won't be picking up the phone to talk to Lisa or Denise or Ana whenever you feel like it."

The ticking became almost unbearable.

"You don't even speak Dutch."

That did it. My mind was made up.

"No," I finally told him, "I'm not going to any country where I can't tell somebody that I want to go home."

As if the wind had been knocked out of him, he let his 6'3" frame collapse into the small, black swivel chair I'd spent hours in while I was studying. With nothing left to say, I crawled into his lap. We hugged each other tightly, and I wept, hanging on to him in the face of having to let go.

The following weeks brought with them a whirlwind of feelings ranging from sadness to disbelief to panic. One week we had been planning our future around Vinz's taking a new job at a luxury hotel that was being renovated; the next, we were sorting our belongings into "his and mine" piles. Unfortunately, the financing on the hotel fell through at the last minute, which brought on his sudden decision to go back to Holland. He hadn't applied for a Green Card, which meant he'd have to find another company that was willing to sponsor his work visa, and he didn't have that. Adding to the pressure-filled atmosphere that had recently moved in, our lease was almost up, and we had nowhere else to go.

It was while we were boxing up the short life we'd built together that I couldn't help but think back to how we'd met. I was no longer sitting in our living room on Jefferson Avenue watching Vinz carrying a box through the kitchen to the garage. I was suddenly transported back two and a half years to the spring of 1997, just months before my thirtieth birthday. I was sitting in The Jefferson Hotel, which was on the corner of 16th and M Streets in D.C.

As my friends and I were all graduate students, the only way we could afford to drink at such a luxurious establishment was if we knew someone on the inside. Dennis the bartender, who'd studied literature with me at the University of Maryland, was our hook up. He'd give us a round of drinks for … a discount.

I'd watched Vinz swagger into the hotel's posh bar, where a couple friends and I had been having a glass of wine.

"Oooh. Who's that tall drink of water?" I'd whispered to Ana, a small feisty Nicaraguan who'd grown up in Miami.

"Ugh, Carolina," she'd responded, her face screwed up with distaste. "The French waiter is so much better looking."

I couldn't have cared less about any little Frenchman; I'd been immediately attracted to Vinz's tall, lean build. His dirty-blond hair had been combed back from his broad forehead, much like Gordon Gekko's in the movie *Wall Street*, but without the asshole quality.

He paused at the bar, where Dennis introduced him to us. I assumed from his accent that he was German, and to break the ice I said, "So, Vinz. What part of Germany are you from?"

"I'm from Holland," he replied in an amused tone that suggested he was used to correcting that mistake.

Feeling comfortable with him, I couldn't resist being a smart aleck. "Eh … Holland, Germany. Same thing." We all laughed. "What brings you to the good ole US of A?"

"I just finished the hotel school in The Hague," he explained. "I came to America to do my internship abroad. The Jefferson offered me a permanent position to manage the bar and restaurant, so I stayed."

Over the next couple of months, Ana and I would drop by the hotel to shoot the breeze with Dennis. If Vinz was on duty, he'd stop and chat and joke around with us. One evening, on a whim, I decided to pop in alone. Dennis motioned to me to take a seat.

"Where's Vinz?" I asked as I situated myself in a tall, leather barstool.

"He called in sick," he said, pouring me my usual glass of wine.

"Mmm hmm," I responded, looking appreciatively at Dennis's face, which was better suited for the cover of a Harlequin romance. He was born in Holland but raised in Spain. He spoke at least four languages. Not only did he have looks and smarts, he was also one of the most down-to-earth people I'd known. And he had a great sense of humor. Out of the blue, he told me he had a confession to make.

"Vinz is crazy in love with you," he whispered conspiratorially. Curious, I leaned in closer and almost knocked over my glass.

"Every time we work together he goes on and on about how beautiful and sexy you are and keeps asking how he can get himself 'some of dat'." Dennis winked and smiled, obviously enjoying himself. "Please put the man out of his misery; put me out of mine for goodness' sake and leave your phone number."

I gave him my number, and, sure enough, Vinz called me a few days later and asked me out. (At least this is the version I tell!)

"Why don't we go rollerblading," I'd suggested to Vinz some time later after we'd gone out a few times. It had been a hot, sunny day, so I figured I'd show him around D.C. my way. Although he'd never rollerbladed before, he had been enthusiastic about giving it a go – or maybe he just wanted to be with me. So, after taking off from his apartment on Connecticut Avenue, we skated through Adams Morgan over to Georgetown. We rested for a few minutes near the corner of Wisconsin and M Streets. I suggested we skate up to the National Cathedral.

"I'm following you," he said.

We trudged up the steep hill and were hot and tired by the time we reached the top.

"Now comes the fun part," I said, wiping the sweat from my forehead.

Vinz grunted and sat down on the curb.

From the top of Wisconsin Avenue, I could see lots of traffic. Obviously, the beautiful weather had inspired Washingtonians and tourists alike to get out and about. Suddenly worried about Vinz's lack of rollerblading experience, I suggested we skate down via the back roads where it was safer for beginners.

"There are a lot of stoplights on Wisconsin," I warned. "You'd be going pretty fast, and it might be hard to stop."

"Carolyn," he said as he adjusted his elbow pads and wrist guards, "I used to ski, and that's all downhill. I think I can manage this." He'd taken off his t-shirt to cool down, and I would have reached out and caressed his chest were it not so sweaty.

"Do you know how to stop?" I prodded.

"I'll be fine," he said, almost tripping over the curb as he stood up.

"Let's go," I shrugged.

"OK, let's do it then."

None too gracefully, he'd made it all the way back down to Georgetown without incident. Until we got to the last stoplight at the bottom of the hill, about a block away from Barnes & Noble. He'd been coasting a bit too fast, and the light turned red too suddenly.

I watched with my hand over my mouth, my brow and nose crinkled up, barely concealing an involuntary "Oooh," as he fell forward and slid under the front bumper of a car that had stopped at the red light.

He had the reflexes of a street hockey player, even if he didn't have the skill. He jumped up, gave the surprised driver the thumbs up and skated over to me.

"Guess I know how to stop," he quipped.

Relieved (and impressed) I laughed as we skated back to his apartment.

The thud of cabinets closing and the soft clang of silverware interrupted my skate down memory lane. My lingering smile gradually faded as the reality of our situation kicked in. While Vinz was in the kitchen packing up our relationship, my thoughts shot back to the first time he cooked dinner for me, shortly before I left him to study in Madrid, Spain. It was the summer 1997 and we were still living in D.C.

"Didn't I tell you I was going to the University of Alcalá to do some research for my dissertation? "I'd said at his look of surprise after casually mentioning that I'd be leaving in a couple of months.

"No, you didn't," he answered, closing the oven door. "You're gonna love Madrid," was all he said.

The mood had turned serious.

"A year's a long time, and we've only been dating a couple of months," I said, no longer hungry for the steak and baked potatoes he was preparing. "What should we do?"

He turned the steaks before replying, "Why don't we decide when the time comes. We still have the rest of the summer. Let's just have fun together."

"Yeah, I agree," I said, relieved, in a way, that he hadn't asked me to blow off my trip. Even though I was falling in love with this tall Dutchman with the twinkling blue eyes, I wasn't ready to give up my dream of going to Spain.

I'd always assumed that since I was fluent in Spanish and was familiar with Latin American literature, I would fit right into the Spanish way of life. Laaawwd – how wrong could I be?

One of the first lessons I'd learned about the Spanish – at least the *madrileños,* or people from Madrid – was that they were language snobs, which didn't go down too easily because I spoke Spanish fluently. Back in D.C. native speakers had had trouble placing my accent. I was variously from Colombia or Panama, even Cuba. Were the *madrileños* impressed with my proficiency? Not in the slightest. They expected me to speak with their accent and had no qualms about correcting mine. It was one thing to correct grammatical errors and quite another to try to change my accent. Was this a black thing? I wondered at first. No, it was a Spanish thing because my dear friend and roommate Claudia, who was also studying in Alcalá, had informed me that comments had been made about her accent. And she was from Argentina.

Because of that, she had been allowed (grudgingly, I expect) to teach beginning-level Spanish to undergraduate exchange students, while I, the non-native-speaking-American, was banished to the Department of Languages' dungeon-like basement with no windows, where I would while away the time waiting to help exchange students struggling with their courses. I tried hard to hold back the indignation because I was, after all, an experienced language teacher preparing for her doctoral exams.

The only positive thing about my "job" was that I had lots of down time. A typical day went something like this: I'd report to the dungeon around 9:30am.

I'd hang out until about 11:00am, chatting with the other graduate students. Then, a group of us would go to a nearby restaurant and eat *tortilla* and crusty bread, drink *café con leche* and smoke cigarettes. We'd go back to the office until about 2:00pm, at which time we'd all return to our rooms for a two-hour siesta. I'd go back around 4:30pm and twiddle my thumbs for another hour before leaving for the day. The whole eight months I was there, I never spoke to one student.

In the meantime my own research had been stymied by the university's Department of Bureaucracy. Before we'd arrived in Spain, Claudia, whose brilliance transcends her doctorate in Latin American literature, had gotten me pumped up to discover a nugget of information that would make my dissertation on the representations of the black female body in nineteenth-century Cuban literature stand out. She was certain there were records about the slave trade in the Spanish National Archives. In the years I'd gotten to know her, I'd come to trust her knowledge, and if she said those records were there, then I believed her. I was determined to let nothing come between me and my nugget. Then again, I hadn't counted on needing an official letter from an "accredited" university verifying my status as a scholar conducting research, which, of course, I didn't have.

So for weeks I walked around the city of Alcalá de Henares trying to get this person to write the letter, that person to sign it and the other to vouch for me. Invariably, she had already left for the day (at 11:00am), he didn't have the authority and they weren't familiar with the procedure, and *por favor, señorita, vuelva Ud. mañana.* "No, I won't come back tomorrow," I felt like screaming. This had gone on for weeks, since, for the Spanish, tomorrow apparently means "in a few days". By the time I got the blasted pass, I was so disgusted with the runaround, it took me another several weeks to get the energy to go to the darned Archives.

Nor were the *madrileños* the warmest of people, even though they affectionately greeted each other with a peck on each cheek. Since they're historically, culturally and even genetically connected to Latin America, I expected them to embrace me as easily as my friends from Mexico, Argentina, El Salvador and Nicaragua had done. But then again, Madrid was a metropolitan, capital city in Europe, and its people weren't exactly famous for their kindness to strangers.

Even New Yorkers tended to be "nicer". On this point I'd had many conversations with other international graduate students there, who uniformly criticized us Americans for being "fake".

"You meet an American and immediately they introduce you as their friend," said a woman from Paraguay on one occasion.

"That's probably because introducing someone as an acquaintance is just too formal," I replied a bit defensively. "I think you're confusing friendliness with an offer of friendship. They're two totally different things. Anyway, what's so wrong with being friendly?" I concluded.

More than once I'd been put off by what I took as rudeness. Walking down the street, for example, I'd said *"buenos días"* to passers-by only to be greeted by blank stares and silence. I'd asked one of my Spanish colleagues down in the dungeon why his people didn't respond to my cheerful smiles.

"Why would you smile at a stranger?" was his response.

I let it go at that.

Probably the worst infraction committed was that the university's administration team had repeatedly gotten between me and my money, and I couldn't have that. I'd show up on payday between 11:00am and 1:00pm (the only time period during which I was guaranteed to speak to a human being ... well ... "guaranteed" being ninety per cent of the time) only to be told my check hadn't come.

"What do you mean my check isn't here?" I'd ask.

"No sé. Pero si puedes volver mañana tal vez cobres."

I was up to here with being told to come back tomorrow and was ready to whoop some Spanish ass.

"Now don't go gettin' all ethnic on 'em, girl. You know you're a guest in their country and ... they still got your money," cautioned the voice inside my head. Not once did I get my measly little pittance of a paycheck on time.

And measly it was. After paying rent at the undergraduate dorm, where Claudia and I were required to live, I had just enough left over for food, a pass for public transportation, laundry and telephone cards. Towards the end of each and every month, I only had a few hundred *pesetas* until payday, whenever that was. That notwithstanding, I hung on to my sense of humor. I could only laugh when Claudia told me once that right before payday she had had to choose between buying a newspaper and a cup of coffee. I told her that I had had to stand at the counter to drink my *café con leche* because sitting at a table cost an extra hundred *pesetas*. We giggled like schoolgirls.

"Well, Carolina," Claudia said, "being poor has one advantage."

I only snorted my reply.

"It's made us creative," she concluded.

And we were. We'd become experts at finding low-cost entertainment. On Sundays, for example, students got free admission into the *Museo del Prado*. I swear, by the end of my stay in Spain, I knew that museum by heart. In order to see Toledo, I volunteered to accompany a group of undergrad exchange students on one of their required excursions to this historic city. I also spent lots of time reading the classics, which were available in abundance in the English section of the university library. On Wednesday nights, I'd walk the ten yards or so to the campus bar and drown my sorrows in cheap wine and dance to music that was already old in the USA. It had its charm. However, after a couple of months, I couldn't help feeling like I was wasting my time. I was thirty years old.

What did I have in common with eighteen-year-old undergraduate students?

Plus, I missed Vinz.

In fact, the highlight of my week was talking to or getting a postcard from him. Despite having agreed to date around while I was away, we'd been keeping in touch regularly. I hadn't even thought about dating. One day after I'd talked to Vinz and was down about not seeing him, Claudia said in that optimistic way of hers, "*Ay, qué bonito, Carolina.*"

"I don't see what's so sweet about it," I said grumpily. "I miss the hell out of him."

"He's courting you with his postcards and phone calls."

I hadn't been able to see past the small but constant irritations to recognize good, old-fashioned courtship, even when it was staring at me right in the face. Even though my research and "cultural education" had come to a standstill, my relationship with Vinz was progressing.

I'd been in Spain about six months when, during one of our phone conversations, Vinz told me about his plans to fly to Holland and surprise his mother on her birthday.

"Wanna fly from Madrid and meet me there?"

As if he needed to ask!

My first impression of Dutch people, made while I had been waiting for Vinz at Schiphol airport in Amsterdam, was that they were a tall lot. I'd been counting on recognizing him by his height, but everybody was tall, so it wasn't until he spotted me that we hooked up. After a long hug and joyful kisses, we hopped on a train and traveled for two hours to his parents' home in Zeeland, a province in the southwest part of Holland.

During the taxi ride to his house, Vinz informed me almost apologetically that the houses in Holland were much smaller than what I'd been used to in America.

If only he knew. I'd grown up in a two-bedroom government-subsidized apartment.

We got out of the taxi about a block from his house so his parents wouldn't get suspicious. Like two kids up to no good, we sneaked up to the house, crawled under the living room window and crouched behind a bush. Vinz picked up a few pebbles and tossed them at the kitchen window, where his mother and brother-in-law were cooking. He grinned when he saw her look up at the kitchen window, startled, before walking to the front door to see what was up.

Her affection had been obvious from the tears welling up in her eyes as she embraced her youngest child and only son. Then she turned to me with a gentle smile and said in her accented but perfect English, "You must be Carolyn," and hugged me with equal affection.

When I walked inside, I felt intimidated because the whole family was there: his father and both his sisters with their husbands and children. It was an unforgettable moment. That week I met most of his childhood and hotel school friends. Just as his family had, they all spoke English to me and welcomed me with open arms. At the end of the week, I was sad to leave him once again to go back to Spain. But I went.

After having spent eight long months in Spain, I moved back to D.C. in the spring of 1998 and found that my lover had actually become my friend. I was happy to be reunited and ready to see where our relationship was heading. Needless to say, I wasn't quite prepared for Vinz's announcement that he'd been offered a position as the director of food and beverage at The Maison Dupuy hotel in New Orleans.

"They want to fly us down for the weekend to see the hotel and meet the head chef," he had told me. "I won't take the job unless you come with me."

I had a few reservations because I'd just spent nearly a year in a country I never really adapted to and wasn't looking forward to another move, even if it was within my own country. On the other hand, I had little to keep me in D.C. besides my friends. I'd already finished my coursework at the university and had been preparing to sit my comprehensive exams. The only thing I needed was a good library. Plus, I wanted to be with Vinz and was intrigued by that city and its chaotic past.

"Let's check it out," I'd said.

$\mathcal{A}$ week before moving to New Orleans, I figured I'd skate one last time with the Washington Area Rollerbladers (or, WAR, as we called ourselves) hoping to see my friend Frank, who had grown up in Tennessee. Luckily, he was at the skating club's meeting point: 1600 Pennsylvania. He was sitting on the sidewalk directly across from the White House lawn smoking a Marlboro Light. I skated over to him, turned off my Walkman and sat down. When I asked him what I could expect as a black woman living with a white man in the South, he studied me silently for a few seconds before answering:

"You'll be OK; you pass the paper sack test." Puzzled, I asked him what the hell a paper sack test was.

"When I was growing up in Tennessee in the 70s," he began, " I had a few black friends. The only ones my mother allowed in the house had skin that was lighter than the brown paper sacks you get at the grocery store."

"Bullshit," I exclaimed skeptically, rolling my eyes at no one in particular.

"That's the South, Carolyn," he concluded almost sadly and stood up. Whether or not it was true, it certainly put me on guard. I'd seen the movies, read the history books and heard stories on the news. I knew the possibilities.

"One other thing," he added as an afterthought, "when you're driving through small towns in Alabama and Mississippi, don't stop if you don't see any stoplights or sidewalks. In fact, make sure you fill up your tank before you leave the big cities." With a look of mischief, he adjusted his earphones and skated away.

The drive down into the Deep South had been tense, to say the least. We'd driven through plenty of small towns, which were generally well equipped with sidewalks and stoplights. New Orleans was the only city south of the Mason Dixon that had ever intrigued me, probably because my mother had been there once when she was younger and had been so impressed by the mixed people she had seen there. She'd told me, her voice filled with wonder, that she'd seen black people with blond hair and blue eyes. Through my graduate research I'd learned that, in its heyday in the eighteenth century, New Orleans had been pretty progressive. It had been the only city in America, before the French sold it that is, where a class of freed slaves and mulattoes were allowed to be educated, work as professionals and own property. Some of them even owned slaves.

What had influenced me the most, however, was *Angel Heart*, the eerie movie starring Mickey Rourke and Lisa Bonet. Set in the 1950s, the movie was rife with historically based stereotypes that cast the city as a haven for illicit voodoo rituals, interracial liaisons and just plain indecency. Can a plot be any more decadent than the devil inducing the main character, a detective hired by the devil to find himself, (huh?) to have sex with his half-breed daughter to get him to acknowledge the grizzly murder he had committed to renege on the sale of his soul? As we drove into the city, I saw that New Orleans had been the perfect setting for all that perversion.

My first impression of the Big Easy was that everything was worn, from the shabby buildings to the raggedy streets. Even the grass seemed dingy to me. It didn't look much different than a scene from *Angel Heart*. I'd been chiding myself for watching too many movies as we pulled into the French Quarter, with its veneer of eighteenth-century European refinement. Alas, as I would come to discover, the wrought iron grillwork decorating the Spanish-style houses and the high-falutin' streets named after the city's French founding fathers didn't quite manage to cover up the thick stench of stale beer nor mask the racial hierarchy that had rendered the city as stagnant as the puddles of rotten water that had accumulated in the gutters.

With all its secrets and mysteries, the *Vieux Carré* was home sweet home until we found a place of our own. We spent the first few weeks learning about this intriguing part of the city. The concierge at the hotel where Vinz had already begun his new job, gave us our first lesson. Linguistics was on the syllabus that evening.

We asked where we might have dinner. His response was to scold us for talking too fast. Then he said, "Ya'll can't walk around here saying *New Orleans*. Around here it's *N'Awlins*."

He finally got around to recommending Commander's Palace, an upscale restaurant that had been a touchstone for fine dining. He'd also informed us that Emeril Lagasse had gotten his start there. We got to Commander's a little later and were shown to our table. We asked the waitress to recommend a good starter, and she suggested, "Bald shrimp; it's always delicious."

"What'd she say?" Vinz whispered as soon as she left to get our menus.

"Bald shrimp," I replied. At his puzzled look I added, "Look, I'm from the Midwest, and we eat regular shrimp there. I guess it's a southern thing."

When the waitress returned, I asked her exactly what bald shrimp was. Her response that it was "just shrimp" didn't clear up the mystery so I asked her how it was prepared. I couldn't quite make out why she looked at me so oddly before answering, "You boil the water and put the shrimp in it," she said.

The light bulb went on. "Ohhh ... *boiled shrimp*," I said, as much to congratulate myself as to explain it to Vinz. It was delicious. But then again, I never ate a bad meal in New Orleans (unless I cooked it myself).

The next day I started looking for a place to live. I was put in charge of that task because my job teaching Spanish at Tulane University wasn't due to start for another couple of weeks. After looking in the paper for a few days, I noticed listing after listing for shotgun houses. I asked the concierge at Vinz's hotel why they got that name. He explained that they were rectangular five-room houses with no hallways. The living room merged into the kitchen, which gave way to a bathroom. Two bedrooms, one on either side of the small house, lay at the back. The bullet from a shotgun would pass through the front door and go straight out the back without hitting anything. I was as intrigued about this novelty of southern living as I was attracted to the low rent, so I called the owner.

After exchanging the appropriate niceties, the owner of the property asked me where I was from and what had brought me to the city.

"I'm originally from Indianapolis, and my boyfriend is Dutch. He's working at a hotel in the French Quarter, and I'll be teaching Spanish at Tulane."

"Have you been to the Latin American library yet?" he asked curiously. He went on to say that he'd put himself through college at Tulane decades before by working in that very library.

I hadn't, but I'd planned to spend many hours there preparing for my comps and researching material for my dissertation. The next few minutes were spent bonding over this common thread in our lives.

"Why don't you come on over tomorrow, darlin', and have a look at the place. I know you'll love it."

The next day found me ringing the doorbell to what I'd hoped would be our new home. The owner opened the front door and his face fell. He'd obviously made the mistake that many others before him had made: he thought the voice on the other end of the line belonged to a white woman. After a limp handshake, he rushed me through the place so fast I felt like . . . well . . . shot from a gun. He whisked me toward the door and began rationalizing why his place wouldn't suit me at all. He proposed I look for a place in some other area of the city (I couldn't recall the name, but it must have been the black side of town).

"You'd feel much more comfortable there," he assured me as he all but pushed me out the door.

So much for Frank's paper sack theory.

Luckily, one of Vinz's employee's mothers was a realtor who was more than happy to help us find a place to stay. We fell in love with the first property she showed us: the bottom unit of a duplex on Jefferson Avenue. Compared to Vinz's apartment in D.C., this place was a palace – space-wise that is. We would have been happy with the spacious living room and separate dining room. When we walked into the kitchen, however, we were blown away. Not only was it big, but it also boasted a breakfast nook. And the two pantries. We could have stored enough food to stock a high school cafeteria. In fact, the two big bedrooms and the den had so many shelves and closets, we had the luxury of filling them with winter clothes, not that we would be wearing them because the climate in New Orleans is subtropical.

Growing up in Indianapolis, I'd been used to hot, humid summers. I hadn't been prepared for nine months of blistering heat in my new city. Damn. It took us a while, but we finally got the hang of it: Vinz and I stopped cycling or rollerblading in the afternoon. On the hottest days, we left the comfort of our air conditioned home to go to work, and that was it. Did the sun have to shine every day? By the time Thanksgiving rolled around, I was fed up. I longed for the crisp days announcing fall. I was tired of sweating and wanted nothing more than to slip into a thick wool sweater. Never a lover of snow, I was nonetheless disgusted by the prospect of celebrating Christmas without it. So, I went back to the Midwest where I just knew I could count on a snowstorm or two. I wasn't disappointed.

More than once I'd heard New Orleans referred to as northern Caribbean as opposed to southern America, and not just because of its intense heat. In 1804 slave rebellions resulted in Haiti becoming the first country in Latin America to declare its independence. To escape the tumult of the revolution, Creoles and free people of color – along with their slaves – fled to New Orleans bringing with them the French language, their religious practices and racial hierarchy. Vodou was a wholly New World creation in which elements of West African and Arawakian religion fused with Catholicism allowing slaves to continue worshiping their gods. But Vodou was more than a religion: it was a means to hold on to an identity that time and space were gradually erasing.

The novelty of the shops in the French Quarter selling sacred objects for voodoo ceremonies as well as tours through cemeteries and histories of voodoo priestesses wore off after our first few months in New Orleans in the face of its outdated racial hierarchy, also imported from the French and Spanish Caribbean plantation societies. In New Orleans Creoles, or local whites, reigned supreme on the social ladder. The more foreign – including northerners – and the darker the person, the lower his/her rung on the ladder. People with unmistakably African features were pushed to the margins of society and culture. I'd been noticing patterns that I had put down to the racial discrimination still prevalent.

Vinz had been hired, not only to manage the restaurant at the Maison Dupuy, but also to raise it up to luxury status. To that end, we'd started frequenting fancy restaurants to check out the competition. I noticed something that bothered me: the wait staff at each of those fancy restaurants was all white. I wouldn't have thought much of it had I not noticed that, at the same time, the bus people were all minorities, mostly black. And that couldn't have been for a lack of qualified black people because there were three historically black colleges right there in town. I'd begun to have second thoughts about living in New Orleans.

And then there was Mardi Gras. Not only was our duplex's location on the corner of Jefferson and Claiborne Avenues convenient to Vinz's job in the French Quarter and my teaching assignment at Tulane University, it was also on the Mardi Gras parade route. I'd seen images on TV of this unique American rendition of Carnival and was thrilled to tick off one more experience I wanted to have before I died. Rather than feeling impressed by this celebration's ability to bring people together to party, laugh and have a merry old time, I was dumbfounded by the segregation it generated.

For two weeks before the famous shebang, a parade would pass by my house, and each day I'd step outside, cross the street and watch. At first the parades were small and mostly limited to marching bands and modest floats. As they made their way up and down the streets on the route, the people riding on the floats, all in costume of course, would toss out to the crowds "throws", which were usually chocolates shaped and wrapped like gold coins or plastic cups emblazoned with the name of the float's krewe. The most prized throws were, of course, the plastic beads, which came in a variety of sizes and, that year, were mostly purple, gold and green.

Krewes, the organizations and social clubs that sponsored a float, were black and white. No, they weren't being watched on an old broke down television set. There was no racial mixing. The white krewes had their floats and the black people had theirs. One afternoon I'd been standing next to a white man who had situated his little girl high atop a lifeguard-type chair so she could enjoy the festivities while he avoided getting a crick in his neck. At the foot of the throne – rather chair – were young black boys running around, just trying to have a good time. Along came a float whose krewe member had been poised to toss a handful of throws. Upon seeing the little white girl and the black boys at her feet, he signaled to the girl's father that his throws were for her and only for her. Hmm, I thought and tried not to make too much of it. The little girl had been awfully cute, and didn't krewe members have the right to throw their throws to whomever they felt like?

A few floats later, though, had me shaking my head in disgust. A few strands of beads landed between the group of black kids and an adult white woman. Obviously not knowing that the beads weren't destined for him, one of the boys grabbed for them at the same time as the woman. Do you know this woman started yelling at this boy and engaging in a tug-of-war with him? Over some beads? That boy couldn't have been more than eight years old and had in no way been threatening. He'd been playing. "Come on, lady!" I wanted to scream. "He's a little boy." I wish I'd have said it. Maybe in some way I could have influenced the situation. On the other hand, I couldn't help but see the scene as a microcosm of race structures in New Orleans and America at large, where "the man", throwing out opportunities and other goods, picked and chose who he wanted to receive them. Blacks and whites, scrounging around on the ground, fought over the leftovers.

By the time our one-year anniversary of living in New Orleans rolled around, I knew in my heart of hearts that I would never be able to settle down there. Not that I'd ever had an inkling of settling down overseas, either, but maybe, just maybe, Vinz's was an auspicious invitation. After so many years being single and longing for a good relationship, didn't I owe it to myself to stoke the flames of this one with the poker of belief that it just might work out? In Vinz I'd found someone I could laugh with and someone with whom I could be me. I was physically attracted to him. He was a man who obviously loved and respected his parents, and most importantly for me his mother, and had been lavishing that same love and respect on me. If I were honest with myself, I'd admit that I had every reason to go with Vinz.

Alas, my head butted in.

"Who do you think you are? This white man is not gonna marry you."

I thought about how black women were depicted on television, in the movies and by the media as loud, skanky welfare ho's kicking up drama with our baby daddies – and that was if we were included at all in America's portrait of itself. Historically, black women had never had the luxury or even the possibility of packing up and running off to "experience the world for a year or two".

But I was being offered that possibility, and I wasn't going to let it pass me by without at least explaining to Vinz why I was so reluctant. So, I walked to the kitchen, where he'd been packing, bent on telling him what was on my mind and in my heart.

"Vinz," I shouted when I didn't find him in the kitchen. "Where are you?"

"I'm in the bedroom."

I walked through the bare den, turned right into the short, narrow hallway leading into our bedroom. Vinz was sitting on the king-sized bed, which, apart from the full-length mirror, was the only furniture we had in there. He looked up from the pile of clothes on the floor in front of him when he heard me coming into the room.

"What's up?" he asked, obviously noticing something was on my mind.

"I just wanted to explain why I'm so hesitant to move back to Holland with you."

I walked a few steps over to the bed and sat down on the gold and maroon patterned comforter my mother had insisted on buying for us last Christmas. I looked into the mirror and saw our reflection. I wondered how two people from such different backgrounds could come together so harmoniously. Looking at my brown skin and curly hair contrasted to his white skin and blond hair, I marveled that we had lasted as long as we had.

To me, his childhood had been idyllic. He had been raised in a stable home with loving parents and two beautiful, older sisters and had never wanted for anything. His father had worked as a manager for a wholesaler of spirits. Using that knowledge and contacts as a springboard, he'd gone on to invest in various businesses, including a snack bar, the Dutch answer to a diner, a restaurant and a hotel, which he owned and ran. Back when Vinz was growing up, Dutch women weren't allowed to work after having children, which, in a backhanded way, was beneficial because Vinz's mother had been at home until he'd started school at four. But his mother hadn't accepted that, and when his father was working his day job, she had run their businesses from home.

To my knowledge, Vinz had never been through anything, so I didn't trust that he'd be strong enough to deal with the eventual fallout of the tragedies that had beset my own childhood. When he was in high school, he and his sister Lyan would spend school vacations working as ski instructors in Austria. He had no student loans, no credit card debt and had been living overseas when he'd met me. Nor did I think he was prepared to deal with the repercussions of dating a black woman. Was he ready for the evil stares we'd eventually get from people who didn't agree with our lifestyle choice? How would he react to snide remarks from people, black and white, who thought we were traitors to our respective races? Could he handle the aggression that lurked in a country as race conscious as America?

Despite our disparate backgrounds, I'd fallen in love with the only man who, up until that point, had satisfied my "list of requirements". I was physically attracted to him. I laughed with him. I respected him as much as he respected me. And, most importantly, I was myself when I was with him. Despite the fact that our sun signs were incompatible – he Gemini, I Virgo – we did share life strategies: we both believed in the power of stepping outside of our comfort zones, and we both subscribed to the notion "live and let live". Deep down we both knew that this move would broaden our horizons in unexpected and unimaginable ways, which was another life philosophy we both submitted to. But was it enough?

Sitting next to him on our bed, I opened the conversation. "More than anything, I'm worried about the racial climate in Holland . . . "

"We have seen black people before, you know," he cut in. "We have people from Suriname, Curaçao, the Dutch Antilles. You know ... the old Dutch empire."

I had to smile at his attempt to reassure me. My research on Caribbean literature had made me sensitive to post-colonial issues. I didn't know if I should be reassured by the fact that the Dutch had taken part in the slave trade, owned slaves and perpetuated the much despised plantation system that I'd planned to deconstruct in my dissertation.

"There are also Indonesians and people from Turkey. Don't worry, there's no racism in Holland."

At my look of skepticism he added, "Well, it's not like it is here in America." As he folded a pair of jeans that he dropped into the open suitcase lying on the carpet next to his foot, he offered, "People in Holland won't care that you're black and I'm white. My family's white, and they really liked you. They always ask about you."

"Yeah, that's because you're not married," the voice in my head replied. Taking up that thread, I blurted out, "I'd like to get married someday." The seconds that passed seemed like hours. "What about you? Do you see marriage in your future?" I asked a bit evasively, not yet daring to look him in the eye.

"Yes, Carolyn. I want to get married some day."

"But would you want to marry me?" I asked bluntly.

He stopped packing and pulled me down onto the bed so that I was lying in his arms.

"Yes. I want to marry you some day," he replied. "Look, I'm going to Holland for good, and I don't think we should get married until you're sure you want to live there. Would you want to have to deal with an overseas divorce?"

It sounded reasonable enough to me.

"How am I going to pay on my student loan? My MasterCard is maxed. Will I be able to work over there?"

"Don't worry about your bills." He looked down at me. "I'll make you a deal. I'll pay off your MasterCard and pay your student loan until you get a job, no matter how long it takes," he said.

I immediately began to relax under the hand that was now stroking my hair. "In case you haven't noticed, Vinz, you ain't got no J.O.B. How are we going to live?"

"Why don't you go back to D.C. while I look for a job in Holland?" he proposed.

Mmm hmm. There it was, the old I'll - go - first - and - send - for - you - later routine.

"When I find something, you can fly over. We can live in The Hague with my sister until we find our own place."

"But what about the language? I don't speak any Dutch so I'm going to be 100% dependent on you to get around. Can you handle that?"

He grinned. "Most people in Holland speak English, Carolyn. It's not like America. We have to learn English and at least one other language in high school. What else?"

I knew I was defeated, but I had one more trump to play. "Who's gonna do my hair?" I smiled at him, satisfied that there was no way in hell this white man was going to have an answer to that one.

"My other sister's a hairdresser."

And out went the fight.

Part II

"Oh come *on!*" I wailed as I looked frantically at the white tank installed on the tiled wall behind the toilet bowl for the metal lever we Americans press gently to flush the toilet. I got down on all fours and desperately felt around the toilet bowl for a button, a knob or a magic wand that would wash away the trail I left in Vinz's friend's small bathroom ... er ... WC (a cubicle with a toilet and a sink). When that failed, I stood up, on the verge of outright panic, turned around and met my face in the small round mirror hanging above the sink that was so impossibly small I couldn't imagine both my hands fitting under the faucet.

"I'm a f*****g Ph.D. candidate. I can *not* believe I can't figure out how to flush this damned toilet."

I felt like throwing myself on the floor, kicking and screaming my frustration at not being able to understand this new world I'd chosen to live in. Instead, I heard my reflection telling me, *"Well, you know what you gotta do."*

I sneered back my response.

We'd been in Holland a couple months when one of Vinz's childhood friends invited us to celebrate his birthday. When we'd arrived at his house, he and his wife were quite welcoming and made the effort to speak English to me. As other guests poured in, the English dwindled and my polite smiles and nods took center stage. I didn't understand what those people were saying. Why was I even faking it? Every time Vinz mentioned my name to a guest, I knew he was explaining our situation and felt like I had to be attentive. Whenever he got up to refill our glasses or to chat with his friend, I freaked out. I'd pretend to be looking urgently for anything in my purse or utterly fascinated with the books in the bookcase so that no one would try to engage me in conversation. Even though my Dutch was non-existent, I was in no mood to decipher broken English. No wonder my intestines were acting up.

So there I was, standing in the WC, prepared to do the unthinkable: walk out of the bathroom, across the kitchen, through the dining room and into a living room full of people, Dutch people I'd never met before, and inconspicuously ask Vinz to come flush the toilet for me. No wonder I felt like a three-year-old. *And* I had to hope and pray no one else needed to use the facilities I'd just marked as my territory!

It wouldn't have been so bad had I simply done a number one. Anyone could be forgiven for not flushing. Don't men do it all the time? Believe me, I wasn't in the habit of doing a number two in random bathrooms. Even before moving to New Orleans, I'd been diagnosed with ulcerative colitis, a chronic digestive condition that left me bound to the toilet. Perhaps due to the stress of so much … well … movement during the previous years, or maybe as a result of my poor eating habits, my body had finally said, "Enough, already." My large intestine had become chronically inflamed, which caused bleeding ulcers. Under such pressure, it stopped performing its function, which was to absorb the fluid from any and all foodstuffs and redistribute it to the rest of my body. Since there was a constant build up of water in my intestines, I had built up an intimate relationship with toilets.

As I washed my hands with ice-cold water (the Dutch don't believe in a warm water tap in the WC), I condemned Vinz to a lifetime of suffering for having brought me to this God-forsaken country. I damned the Dutch culture for having devised more ways to flush a toilet than there are ways to skin a cat. In short, I cursed every decision I had made that led me into this wretched situation. I sucked my teeth, dried my hands and opened the door. I walked out of the WC, ready to meet my fate.

I never made it out of the kitchen. My hostess was standing at the table assembling various smelly French cheeses, sausage and crackers. "You found the WC?" she smiled as she asked, completely oblivious to my terror. Little did she know, she was rescuing me from complete social humiliation.

I mustered up the courage to tell her my problem. "I can't flush the toilet." She advanced towards the WC with a chuckle.

"*NO*," I all but shouted, "just explain it, I'll do it myself."

I walked back into the WC and saw it: the chain. Of course … the chain that I had thought was a part of the tank. I yanked it with everything I had and the waters of relief flushed over me.

And then, in the words of Terry McMillan, I exhaled.

$\mathcal{B}$efore leaving the US for Holland a few months before, Vinz, true to his word, had arranged for us to live in The Hague with his oldest sister Annick, her husband Wouter and their three boys, Tim aged eleven, Nick nine and Pieter eight. When he'd first informed me of this arrangement, I couldn't help but express my displeasure in the form of nagging questions: How long would we have to stay there? What were those kids like? How were four adults going to live together under one roof? What I was really feeling was fear at how they would react to having a black woman living in their house. When I brought it up, Vinz's only response was, "It's Holland, Carolyn, not America."

From day one, they treated me as part of their family, never asking me to lift a finger to do anything. They didn't care that I was black or American, for that matter. Wouter, who had lived in England, would give me a hard time about my accent and pronunciation. He would refer to me as a "bloody American" when

I didn't understand the Queen's English, which he spoke. I was from Indiana, how should I know what a "dustbin" was? Since we were the only two who smoked, we'd go outside after dinner and chat. I discovered an ally in Wouter.

Pieter, their youngest son, had agreed to bunk with the middle brother Nick, so out came his twin bed and in came a queen-size mattress that virtually covered the entire floor of that oh-so-cramped space we'd be calling our bedroom for the time being. Since the average Dutch bedroom does not come equipped with a built-in closet, we cleared the poor boy's shelves of all his toys and used them to store our clothes.

During the day the kids were at school and Vinz, Annick and Wouter were at work. I had the house to myself, which was a gift considering I'd always needed lots of me-time. Why hadn't I brought my cross-stitching, though? It certainly would have made sitting on the couch watching reruns of *Matlock* and *As the World Turns* more bearable. Unfortunately, I'd had it shipped along with all the other personal stuff I'd deemed "nonessential". How was I supposed to know I'd be waiting nearly three months for my stuff? On the other hand, I was grateful that all foreign programs on Dutch television were broadcast in their original language accompanied by subtitles. I had had the foresight, however, to bring a few books and articles with me on the plane. So, after *Matlock* beat the bad guys in court, I could at least go through the motions of furthering my dissertation.

It was early December and cold outside. Inside I couldn't figure out how to turn the heat up, so I froze. My hosts kept the room temperature at a chilly sixty-six degrees, so I took to wrapping myself in a blanket to keep warm. Alas, sitting alone in a cold house trying to read and take notes with a blanket that drooped off my shoulders every time I turned a page was awkward, to say the least. It was also a far cry from the intellectually stimulating discussions I'd had back in the States – in Spanish to boot – with my Mexican, Salvadorian and Argentine roommates. How I ached to be standing in front of a classroom teaching a group of undergraduates, even though I preferred doing anything other than learning how to conjugate verbs. I sorely missed meeting up with my colleagues at the student union and complaining about this professor or that seminar over a slice of pizza and a Coke. I was so desperate; I would have gladly moved back to New Orleans because, at least there, Vinz and I were on equal footing and only had each other.

As it was, *he* had his family around him. *He* could move around easily in the country and culture *he'd* grown up in. *He* spoke the language. *He* had a job. *He'd* even had the nerve to go skiing for a week with his buddies from the hotel school. We'd only been in Holland a month or so and off he went to France for a week, leaving me alone in a cold house with his family. I was fuming. Most of all, though, I was sad because I wanted nothing more than to talk to Monika and Michelle, my childhood friends, but I couldn't. I had neither the guts nor the privacy to make long international calls on my in-laws' phone. With a six-hour time difference, the only chance I had to call was in the evening when the house was full.

Alternately, I felt like an ungrateful little wretch for indulging in self-pity, which was often during those first few months. There I was living in Europe with the love of my life. Since I wasn't working, I had the time to explore my new country or at least pour myself into my studies. I was living out the dream of so many women, and still I wasn't satisfied. I needed to take a few steps, no matter how small, towards creating a fulfilling experience, but I didn't know how to do that when I couldn't even figure out how to turn the heat up.

"Bruce Lee's on TV tonight," Vinz proclaimed one Saturday evening, determined to show me that, on some fronts, Holland was no different from America. We'd taken to leaving his sister's house on Friday after Vinz got home from work to spend the weekend in the relative quiet of his parents' lakeside home in the province Zeeland, about an hour and a half from The Hague. I was ecstatic. I loved Bruce Lee. In fact, I'd actually taken my first trip abroad with my mother . . . at the drive-in . . . in Indianapolis. She used to take my sisters and me to see karate pictures, which really meant Bruce Lee movies. We were so excited. We had our big paper sack of home-popped popcorn with grease stains all over it and a couple cans of grape pop. We'd go early to get a front row "seat" and a speaker that worked. I was the youngest, so my place in the car was in back behind my mother. I may have lost out on the bid to sit up front, but I had the honor of sticking my gangly brown arm out the window and grabbing the speaker with my long, piano player's fingers. For the rest of the evening, I was in control . . . of the volume.

I'd probably seen every Bruce Lee movie at least six times each, but my favorite was *Chinese*

Connection, probably because it was the only movie in which he actually kissed my favorite co-star, Nora Miao, who always looked so demure even though she sure could kick some ass. I'd been so enamored with what I thought was Chinese culture that I made up my mind to learn Chinese and live in China with Bruce and Nora. I'd even borrowed the "C" encyclopedia from a neighbor and got to work. Good thing I couldn't be bothered to read the pages-long entry dedicated to a country I'd only heard about in the black-man-white-man-Chinese-man jokes told by the neighborhood kids because, as I found out twenty years later, Bruce Lee was from Hong Kong!

Set during the period when Shanghai and surrounding coastal territory were under foreign occupation, the movie's plot was deceptively simple. Chen Zhen, Bruce Lee's character, returns to his martial arts school just in time to see his teacher being buried, having died mysteriously. Later, two students from the rival Japanese school interrupt the eulogy to taunt the Chinese with a sign that reads "Sick man of Asia". While holding vigil over his teacher later that evening, Chen Zhen overhears two kitchen workers. When one admits to poisoning Teacher with a plate of cookies, Chen Zhen jumps out of the shadows to confront them. When he sees from their undergarments that they're Japanese spies who have infiltrated the school, it's on. He pins one of the offenders to the wall and growls, "Why did you kill my teacher then?" And when he refuses to answer, Chen Zhen roughs him up and repeats, "Why did you kill my teacher then? Why, why, why, why, why, why, why?" each "why" being accentuated with a deadly karate chop to the belly.

One of the most poignant scenes is when Chen Zhen attempts to enter a public park after secretly paying a visit to the Japanese school to return the offensive sign. An Indian official guarding the entrance stops him and then points to a sign reading: "No Chinese or dogs allowed."

"But, if you get on your hands and knees and bark," laughs the official viciously, "maybe this nice couple will take you in."

The crowd scoffs. Chen Zhen looks at the sign. His face screws up. He bellows out an impassioned *hiiii yaaahhh* (as only Bruce Lee can do), and jumps into the air. With one foot he kicks the offensive piece of trash sign and breaks it in half with the other foot. At the end of the movie, before Chen Zhen sacrifices himself before an angry firing squad, he proclaims to his oppressors: "We are not sick men."

Unbeknownst to me at the time, *Chinese Connection* would loosely parallel one of the major issues that would unravel as I fought my way through the tragedies that would define my childhood. I certainly knew a thing or two about feeling powerless in one's own land. As it was, watching Bruce Lee's mesmerizing brown eyes, elegant hands, and the way his body moved so gracefully had distracted me from the limitations I was told my own body would place upon me.

When Chinese slippers came out – the flat black cloth shoes with a cement-colored rubber sole and a thin strap that buckled over the bridge of your foot – I had to have a pair, and every time I put them on I became someone other than who my mother, the black community and white America told me I was.

How many times had my mother informed me: "Carolyn, you're poor, black and a girl," slamming the fist of one hand into the palm of her other hand as she said those last three words?

"You've got three strikes against you right off the bat," she'd add just in case I didn't get it the first ten times.

I suppose that had been her way of preparing me for the world as she had been taught to see it. But she didn't really have to because I had my Chinese slippers, and whenever I wore them, I imagined myself speaking a language no one in my neighborhood could understand and whooping anybody's ass who got up in my face. Whenever I wore my Chinese slippers, I was prepared for the world as I was learning to see it.

By this time that world had become unrecognizable. I was surrounded by the foreign sounds of a language I didn't understand, I'd been plopped down in a culture whose codes seemed undecipherable and imprisoned by a lifestyle that I hadn't yet developed the skills to change. I'd begun to feel like I'd been broadsided by a MACK truck. Some people have comfort food; I was looking forward to a comforting TV experience. While Vinz's mother was in the kitchen making coffee, tea and sweet nibbles, I snuggled into her red suede recliner, with a little smile of anticipation. A winsome feeling of home overcame me as the haunting opening theme and credits flashed across the widescreen TV.

My heart dropped like a ton of bricks upon hearing the first spoken words a minute or two later. Like all foreign movies in Holland, *Chinese Connection* was broadcast in its original version: Cantonese with Dutch subtitles. Unbelievable. Apparently, the Dutch didn't realize that half the fun of watching these movies was the fact that the characters' mouths were not synchronized with the dubbing. Vinz and his mother, bless their hearts, tried not to laugh. They weren't successful. I rolled my eyes and, with a huff, got up and grabbed my book on post-colonial literature. I sat on the couch and held it up to my face pretending to read, all the while snickering. I too saw the humor.

Back in The Hague a couple of weeks later, I'd gotten tired of feeling down and being cloistered, so I worked up the courage to venture out to the *centrum*, or downtown area. Excitement, and, dare I say, relief, bubbled up inside me as I walked to the tram stop, following my sister-in-law's directions. It was early afternoon when I boarded the tram and bought a ticket from the conductor, who, by the way, spoke English. After about twenty minutes, we pulled into The Hague's *Centraal Station*, and I got off the tram.

It was a beautiful, sunny winter's day, so I was looking forward to a brisk walk into town. The nice man sitting behind the information desk assured me it was a seven-minute walk straight ahead. My heart started beating faster as I walked through the *Plein*, or town square, where people were sitting outside on restaurant terraces warmed with heat lamps, sipping midday cocktails, chatting and just enjoying the beautiful weather. I wasn't brave enough to sit by myself so I kept walking. Out of the corner of my eye, I saw a massive yet quaint building.

Hmm, what is that? I wondered to myself as I deviated momentarily from my shopping plans and walked toward what I later discovered was the *Mauritshuis*, an art museum that is home to paintings by Vermeer and Rembrandt and other Dutch masters. I would have gone in, but my attention was again distracted by a passage, opening in front of the museum. I followed the other people through it and caught my breath. I was standing in a medieval courtyard complete with a statue as its centerpiece and an impressive archaic clock tower. Old buildings, literally from the Middle Ages, bounded the courtyard. I'd stumbled upon the *Binnenhof*, center of Dutch politics, where the prime minister keeps his offices and where the House of Representatives holds its sessions.

Every September on *Prinsjesdag* the Dutch queen enters the courtyard in a gilded carriage pulled by a team of horses and holds her annual state-of-the-union-type address in one of those medieval buildings, the *Ridderzaal*. My excitement changed into euphoria as my clunky heels clopped over the cobblestones, carrying me through time toward the shopping area. Here I was, all by myself, taking in the sights and atmosphere of a cosmopolitan government city, which reminded me a lot of Washington, DC.

As I walked into this boutique and out of that cute little shop, I couldn't be disappointed by the absence of a shopping mall *à la Americaine*. In fact, in those couple of hours, I felt myself bonding with The Hague, an unlikely cohort in my first step toward self-sufficiency. I congratulated myself as I made my way back to *Centraal Station* and hopped back on tram number two, my confidence riding high. After about twenty minutes, I got hit in the face with the realization that I had no clue where to get off. The scenery at my tram stop, that I just knew I'd recognize, was as foreign as I was. Why didn't I write down the name of the stop? I got off at a familiar-looking stop, but then again, don't all sidewalks and grassy fields look the same?

Vinz had written down his sister's address and phone number for me, which, luckily, I had with me but they were both useless. No one was home so I couldn't call, and if I knew how to find the address written on the paper, I wouldn't be lost, would I? I'd been wandering around for what felt like hours trying to find some recognizable landmark. By the time I saw a police station, I was on the verge of panicking.

"Oh, hell *no ... you're not about to ask the police ... the police ... to take you home. You're a thirty-one-year-old woman,"* said that voice in disbelief. *"How are you supposed to ask the police officer where you live when you don't even know how to say 'where do I live' in Dutch?"* that voice taunted.

Resigned to my fate, I muttered, "This is some bullshit," before heading to the main doors of the police station and then shuffling over to the woman sitting at the nearest desk.

"Excuse me, Ma'am," I managed to squeak out, hoping she'd understand me. "I'm lost," I said, barely managing to keep the sarcasm from my voice. "Could you help me find this address please?" I reached into my pocket and pulled out the crinkled sheet of notebook paper, feeling like a five-year-old.

She smiled reassuringly and looked at the address. She stood up and walked outside with me. She managed to explain, in English, that I was just a few blocks from where I needed to be. By the time I got back, it was early evening and Vinz and my in-laws (and the kids) were sitting at the dining room table.

"Where have you been?" said Vinz, signs of worry marking his face as he kissed me.

By the time I told my story, I realized how ridiculous it sounded. My chuckles turned their smirks into outright laughter. Hours later as I lay on the mattress next to Vinz in that cramped room, I felt a rush because I'd managed to do something. Even though I'd gotten lost, I'd taken a few steps away from feeling sorry for myself.

Looking back at those first six months in Holland I realize my culture shock had been as much a reaction to feeling broadsided by my loss of independence as to the Dutch culture. I felt helpless, and that contradicted the image of a strong, independent black woman that my mother had pounded into my head as I was growing up. She used to tell me that I couldn't be as good as white people. "You have to be better, Carolyn," she'd say.

When I got older I figured out that that had been her way of preparing me to live in what she called "a white man's world". She didn't have to bother with words because my childhood, which was worthy of a statistic, had given me no other choice but to be strong. Cory, Dawn and Felicia, my brother and sisters, and I were raised in a government-subsidized apartment complex by a single mother and no reliable father figure. When I think back to how little we had, I wonder how we survived on the salary my mother made as a secretary. Now, it's funny when I think back to when we told all our friends that we were vegetarians, which we technically were though not by choice. We just couldn't afford to buy meat on a regular basis. Or vegetables, for that matter. We had a stable diet of grits and rice. So I suppose the more appropriate term would have been grits-and-rice-atarians.

We must have made it on my mother's survival wisdom, which I always believed was inherent in black women. For example, the last few days before payday were always the tightest so my mother would slip a roll of toilet paper from the restroom at work into her purse or steal a few dollars from the office coffee fund, with which my oldest sister, Felicia, somehow whipped up a meal.

I once had told Vinz about the time Dawn carried me on her back to the store (probably to buy grits or rice) because I didn't have any shoes. I longed for a pair of those light brown earth shoes with the square toe and cool white stitching across the top. I knew if I asked my mother for the twenty dollars to buy them, she'd tell me she didn't have the money. She'd say she only had ten dollars to last until payday, which is what she always said when we asked for money.

She'd been upstairs with Dawn and Felicia one Saturday afternoon so I knew the coast was clear downstairs where her purse sat open and unattended. I crept over to the sagging couch and slowly, ever so slowly, stuck my hand in and pulled out her wallet, trying not to touch anything for fear of setting off an alarm like in that game Operation. She had a whole bunch of twenties, so I was sure she wouldn't miss one. (How was I supposed to know she had put aside those twenty-dollar bills to pay the rent?) I took one, walked up to Fayva Shoe Store, and bought my shoes. It never even crossed my mind that she might wonder where I suddenly got a new pair of shoes, but she didn't say a word . . . until a few days later.

She'd been in a rage, walking around the living room talking to herself. "What's wrong," I asked.

"I'm missing twenty dollars."

I'd hoped my guilt didn't show as I looked down and saw her $20 on my feet. To my utter amazement she said, "I bet I know who took my money. That bitch Audrey at work must've gone in my purse when I was in the bathroom."

She went on walking around the living room muttering to herself. Me and my earth shoes strutted out the back door. I never thought about it again.

Ironically, it had never occurred to me that we were poor because we seemed to have more than many of the kids in our apartment complex. However, the first time I did become conscious of our poverty was the afternoon when a white woman came with her white daughter from some nearby church to donate some canned food they'd collected. I never recalled the words that were spoken, but I was aware of the absurd silences between the polite small talk. There we stood around our beat up dining room table: the blonds and the brunettes; the white, the brown and the light skinned looking at one another. Not even words could put us on common ground. As I looked over that little white girl dressed in her cute little cotton dress, I felt like I was wearing poverty the same way as I wore my brown skin and little girl's body.

To be sure, that legacy of survival wisdom had skipped a generation because I was in Holland struggling. I couldn't do something as simple as walk into the bakery around the corner and order a loaf of the fresh, warm bread that I could smell through my future in-laws' windows, which were always left cracked no matter how cold it was outside. Since I didn't speak the language, I couldn't read signs. So, when my one pair of good shoes needed to be resoled, I didn't bother to read the hand-written sign posted on the door. Since I didn't read Dutch, I assumed the information contained in the notice didn't pertain to me.

I went back a couple days after dropping off my only pair of good shoes to find that the shop was closed. I knew that on Sundays everything was closed, but it was the middle of the week. Why weren't they open? I all but stood there with my nose pressed against the window, looking desperately for my shoes, as if seeing them on a shelf somewhere would magically pick the lock.

The handwritten sign on the door, which I'd ignored a couple days before, hung there taunting me. I looked closer, and a few words stuck out: vacation and closed. I couldn't believe it. The shop had closed for two weeks. What kind of business would close its doors for two friggin' weeks with my shoes locked inside? I was in a rage, and later that day, I went off on Vinz for committing the cardinal sin of being Dutch. His calm explanation (and dig on American culture) that Dutch people were actually allowed to use their vacation days only fueled the fire.

"What's up with you?" he asked, clearly not understanding what I was going through. "Go out and buy another pair."

"That's not the point," I shot back nastily. "They could've said something when I dropped the shoes off."

"Well, that's why they put the sign on the door."

I wanted to tell Vinz exactly what he and the shop owner could do with that lousy sign. But he was right. I was just venting my frustration at being confronted with so many differences in my daily life. Before moving to Holland, I had earned my own money and paid my own bills. I had my own apartment. I had my own life. Most importantly, I knew who I was. Being in Holland was forcing me to question everything that I thought defined me as an adult. Being in Holland, I sometimes felt powerless, and I hadn't felt like that since 1977, the year I turned ten and when the first of many tragedies struck my family.

Cory had been ten years older than me, and before I ever really knew him, he'd enlisted in the army and was stationed in Germany. I remembered him coming home every now and then, playing *Monopoly* with my sisters and me and giving us a little spending money. Because Dawn had shown promise as a gymnast, he'd offered her one dollar for every back handspring she could do in a row.

She got *ten* dollars! For me, he used to put on a record and sing this song:

I'm happy to see you again (bom bom bom)
I'm happy that you are my friend (bom bom bom)
I haven't seen you for a long, long time (shoo be do)
I'm happy to see you again.
Happiness is seeing a friend, seeing a friend again
Happiness is singing a song so won't you come on
and sing along

You know I'm happy to see you again
(shum shum ba de ba)
Happy that you are my friend (bom bom bom)
I haven't seen you for a long, long time (shoo be do)
Happy to see you again

I may not remember much of Cory, but I'll never forget him, bent down on all fours, bouncing up and down, serenading me as I sat on the couch squealing with laughter. I have no idea who sang that song, and since my recent efforts to dig up the artist have failed, I'm beginning to wonder if it ever existed. Was Cory making it up as he went along, improvising to imprint in his mind his baby sister's laughter, something lightweight that took up little space; something he would unpack when he flew back overseas?

How is it possible to remember every word of a song, even the background vocals, yet barely recollect the person who, unknowingly, bestowed upon me my own special remembrance of him? Cory died shortly after singing it to me, and now my memory of him comes only as blurry vignettes spliced together with all the tears my mother cried for him through all the years of my life.

The summer of 1977 he'd just turned twenty. He'd taken leave from the army because my mother had gotten "sick" and needed his help. One scorching afternoon in July he dropped me, Dawn and Felicia off at a nearby swimming pool and said he'd be right back. Although we begged him to stay and swim with us, he told us to be good and then left.

We never saw him again.

The next thing I recall is sitting on the kitchen counter and somebody telling us that Cory had been stabbed. The story we'd been given by my uncle Russell, my mother's youngest brother who was with Cory when it had happened, was that he'd fallen on the knife while playfully wrestling about with "a few other cats". My mother had always suspected that somehow my uncle had been involved, and from that day forward she barely spoke to him.

Years later, or maybe it was months or weeks after his death, Felicia told me how she remembered seeing our mother in the intensive care unit holding our only brother's listless hand, chanting, "I love you I love you I love you I love you I love you I love you." Because I was so young and wasn't allowed to see him or say goodbye, I can only imagine this scene: him dying in a hospital bed with tubes coming out of everywhere (or maybe they were going in everywhere) and the plug being pulled on my distraught mother. Cory had been her respirator, and when he died she had nothing to keep her alive. Not even us girls.

Years later, I would be left wondering how someone I had hardly known could change my life irreversibly. I would never know that person who had stolen my mother from me when I was only ten years old. I would end up spending a lifetime mourning a stranger, and even though I would never find out exactly what led to his death, I would come to understand that my life had been downgraded into a nostalgic possibility. From that day on I would always wonder how the constant presence of a strong, black male might have changed my life.

I don't recall ever mourning Cory's death. We never discussed it. In fact, shortly after it had happened, my mother took my sisters and me to stay in her childhood home with Grandma Thelma for a while because she couldn't take care of us. We did not like Grandma Thelma. She scared us. She was a hard woman who'd never been free with her affection. In fact, my mother was, for the most part, raised by her grandmother, so it wasn't hard to understand why they'd had such a rocky relationship. My mother had once confided in me that after Cory had been stabbed, Grandma Thelma had come to the hospital to sit with her. Across my brother's deathbed, their eyes met, and in that look my mother had felt all the love, compassion and understanding that she'd never gotten growing up. Though no words were spoken, she'd felt close to her mother for the first time in her life.

Before I was even born, my grandmother had had a stroke, which had left her almost paralyzed on one side. She carried one arm as though it were in a sling, and she used the other one to hold on to her three-pronged metal walker with big black rubbers on the bottom of each prong. She couldn't stand Felicia, who, according to her would always cause my mother heartache. She tolerated me. After I was born, she'd told my mother, "She's pretty, but don't have any more." She adored Dawn. But then again, everybody adored Dawn.

The three of us would spend most of our time that fateful summer cooped up together in the big bedroom facing Ethel Street. I was standing in that bedroom with my sisters, watching our grieving mother get in her light blue Buick Regal and drive away. I didn't understand why she was leaving us behind, and I ached to go with her. Instead of having an opportunity to mourn our brother's death with our mother, my sisters and I had spent the following months creating opportunities to liven up our miserable days.

Because she was the fastest, Dawn would jump out of that bedroom window, sprint down to the corner store and bring back bags of sweet, joyful distractions from the hours of missing our mother and not really understanding why she left us with our mean grandmother who called us hussies when she got mad at us. We were tight then; we had to be because we only had each other. Little did we know back then, we wouldn't have each other much longer.

That summer we spent our days watching television in our grandmother's bedroom. My favorite shows were *Josie and the Pussycats* and *Wait Till Your Father Gets Home*. In the evening, when the TV went off, we tried to stay out of trouble, which we managed to do, until the night I almost burned down the house.

The there of us were in our little bedroom, and Dawn and Felicia were striking matches. I wanted to strike one too, but my sisters told me I was too young. I just got to watch. Until their backs were turned. I snagged a book of my own and disappeared under the bed, lest they see what I was up to. From where I lay on my belly, I noticed a corner of the sheet of our unmade bed dangling over the side and wondered what would happen if I lit it. I soon found out I yelled for Dawn and Felicia to come help me put it out but the fire had already spread. We managed to put it out, but not before the bed had been destroyed and the room filled with smoke.

We knew we were in trouble so we climbed out of the window and headed up Ethel Street, at night, toward our Aunt Carrie's, who was one of Grandma Thelma's sisters. We didn't get much farther than one block before Felicia, whose idea it was to run away, confessed to not knowing exactly where Aunt Carrie lived. We went back to face the music, played to the stinging tune of Grandma Thelma's extension cord. Not surprisingly, we went back home shortly after that.

Despite falling into a deep depression following the death of her oldest child and only boy, my mother had to work; somebody had to pay the rent. Felicia, four years older than me, had to pick up most of the slack at home. She'd go to the store, cook and clean. Dawn and I had to pack up whatever bits we could find for our school lunch. We washed our own clothes, combed our own hair and did just about everything else, short of earning money. From somewhere, my mother had found the strength to keep going.

My earliest memories of her were of a stunning woman who may have laughed every now and then but never smiled. But then, I guess she didn't have much to smile about. She was born in Indianapolis in 1936. When she was eight or nine her parents were divorced. Apparently, at that time, the labor market in Indiana couldn't accommodate a single black mother, so Grandma Thelma found a job in Washington, DC.

For two years she left my mother with her grandmother Estella who was, according to my mother, heavy-set and dark-skinned. "She was the sweetest woman in the world to me," my mother recollected. "I really loved her a lot."

My mother had grown up in the house on 27th and Ethel, which was built by one of her uncles in what is now considered the inner city of Indianapolis. Right up the alley had been a beauty shop where my mother had gone regularly to have her hair straightened out. She'd been struck by a picture of a Native American woman that hung on the wall and had told me that she remembered praying that her hair would turn out as long and straight as that racially ambiguous woman's.

She was positive that her views of race had been set during those years. Indeed, the most influential women in her life had instilled in her a hatred of dark-skinned people with nappy hair. As my mother tried to pass that same nonsense along to my sisters and me, she would illustrate the lesson with stories of her elementary school travails. One little girl, for example, had come up to her and socked her in the face. Another little girl, Jackie, used to follow my mother home at lunchtime for one reason only: to kick my mother's ass. As my mother told it, those girls had had three things in common: they were black, nappy-headed and ugly.

Her mother and grandmother hadn't allowed her to attend Crispus Attucks, the black high school. No, they forced her and her oldest brother to go to Shortridge, where she had been the only black in her graduating class. She'd often talked about the Jewish girl she sat next to, who tacitly reminded her of her lowly place on the social ladder.

"Her father owned the Pels Dance Shop," she would drone, staring vacantly into the space next to me. "Everyday she came dressed in a different outfit. Her pocketbook and shoes always matched. I was so embarrassed because I had to wear Thelma's old dresses."

"I was so lonely," she'd once confided to me, " because no one at Shortridge talked to me."

So while my mother experienced discrimination from the white people at school, her family taught her to discriminate against blacks. She grew up believing she was "better" than most black people because she had "good" hair, light skin and family members who'd reached prominence in their careers. Alas, not even those privileges could inoculate her from the explicit racism that was prevalent in Indianapolis at the time. She swore that at the entrance of the segregated Broad Ripple Park, now the artsy-fartsy, cultural section of the city, stood a sign that read: "No Niggers Allowed".

Grandma Thelma had forced my mother into court reporting after she'd graduated from high school because, as my mother told it, my grandmother wasn't going to take care of any babies. Reluctantly, my mother learned stenography but, in a moment of defiance, got pregnant with my brother. My grandmother made my mother marry Bill Starks, a handsome man with light skin and gray eyes. Shortly after Felicia Ann was born, six years later, the marriage was over. Bill had become so jealous and possessive of my mother that he'd taken to following her around.

"That man'll end up killing you, Beverly," my grandmother warned, so my mother divorced him.

In the two years that followed, my mother had met and married my father, David Vines, and given birth to Dawn Yvette. They'd moved to Toledo, Ohio, where he'd grown up with his nine brothers and sisters. He'd been tall and athletic and had an easy smile. He'd once shown me a picture of himself at nine or ten posing with a professional baseball player. His big smile and bushy eyebrows were imprinted in my memory, mainly because Dawn had been a carbon copy of him. I came along two years later while my father had been finishing his master's degree in education and my mother had been commuting to Detroit after work to attend evening classes in stenography.

By the time I was five, my parents' marriage was over. My mother divorced him, and on the advice of my grandmother, she took us kids back to Indianapolis, leaving a promising career as a court reporter. To make ends meet, she'd been sent out by Manpower on temporary secretarial assignments until she got a permanent position at the Federal Probation Office in downtown Indianapolis.

She hated that job, but it was better than going on welfare, like so many other women in her position had done. After working all day, she'd come home and spend hours practicing her court reporting. One of the few vivid images I have of the mother of my childhood was her sitting in a chair in the dining room, fingers flying over the blank, black keys of her stenograph, her brown eyes staring at nothing in particular.

I never knew what was worse for my mother: the disappointment at not being able to fully support her family or the resentment at having to do secretarial work under the supervision "a dumb white woman". How many times had I heard those words when my mother was encouraging my sisters and me to get good grades and go to college so we'd never have to go through what she went through? A big part of her identity must have been wrapped up in being a court reporter because, when she was in the courtroom, she got respect. She was more than just the negative images America had attached to a black woman.

In the years that followed, my mother struggled to put our lives back together. From somewhere she had found the strength to pursue her dream of getting back into the courtroom she'd loved so much. I don't think she was very successful, but how could she be when the essential piece of the puzzle had been lost? In the years that followed, I was making some transitions of my own. I was entering puberty and junior high school, leaving behind the little kid years. Shortly before the beginning of 7th grade, I found out that I wouldn't be attending the junior high school up the street from where we lived. I was being bussed to the predominantly white Northview Jr. High in the rich, white part of town. I didn't understand the politics behind desegregation, but I did understand my fear at being separated from my sisters. I could only silently question what those white people were going to do to me. Up to that point in my life, I'd had very little direct contact with white America, so it was natural that I'd want to know who was going to have my back.

Ultimately, there had been no race riots at Northview, and our Vice-Principal was a black man, so all of my worries had been unfounded. I relaxed and started enjoying myself. I found my own way, without Dawn and Felicia, and while I didn't make any significant friendships with any of the white kids, I learned they weren't out to get me, either. My guidance counselor was supportive and my teachers seemed to take a liking to me, especially my Spanish teacher. To her face we all called her Señorita Wagner but, under my breath I called her Saint Doris.

Every morning her Farrah Fawcett hair came bouncing into class followed by her mile-a-minute jibberish that in time would become my second language. Miss Wagner had been in love with two things: Purdue University and all things Spanish, especially Josele Garza, a famous racecar driver. We were all in love with her. She taught us how to play "Olé", which was her made-up version of "BINGO". She organized in-class talent shows, in one of which

Tina and Pamela, the other two black girls, and I sang
a soul version of "Are You Sleeping Brother John" in
Spanish. Not too many other kids growing up in the
projects could say that. For an upcoming Parent Day,
she asked us all to prepare a Spanish dish, so I stole
a dollar from my mother's purse to buy a package of
shredded coconut, the main ingredient in *cocadas,*
candies made by boiling water, adding sugar, and
stirring in the coconut. When I bit into the first one I
thought I had just swallowed a cup-full of sugar, and I
was sucking the coconut out of my teeth for the rest of
the day. To this day I can't stomach coconut, but I still
love me some Spanish.

On the first day of class, Miss Wagner went
around the classroom and one by one gave us our
new names, flicking her feathered hair as she did it.
My friends Tina and Pamela had it easy. They didn't
really have to say their names differently in Spanish.
But when she got around to me and said "Te llamas
Carolina" my heart started pumping gallons of blood
through my body, my eyes got big and my fingernails
found their way to my teeth. I was too embarrassed
to say my new Spanish name. I hated telling people
my name in English. It was such a long and proper-
sounding name. To most of the people, kids and

some adults, the three syllables in my name had been reduced to two: Curlyn. Every time I said "Carolyn" I just knew people were silently accusing me of "talking white".

So there I was, the center of attention, asked to pronounce four syllables and roll my "R". Miss Wagner insisted, firm but kind, that I say my name. "Carolina" was born that day. And whenever I was called on to answer a question, I spoke a language no one else in my little world spoke; whenever I spoke Spanish, I knew I was prepared for the new world I was about to see.

During that first year of Spanish class, I thought I was unique. I believed I was the only one in my family to have ever studied it, until my mother confessed that she, too, had had a secret love of the language. We weren't Catholic, although we did attend an Episcopalian church from time to time when my mother got tired of the Baptist church, but her solemn confession of her high school Spanish connection would have earned her a couple years' worth of credit in heaven.

"I took Spanish I in high school, but I just didn't understand it," she'd told me. "I would have flunked, too, if the teacher hadn't given me a D."

My undivided attention caught, I'd asked her how she'd passed if she hadn't known anything.

"My teacher had made me promise never to take another Spanish class again."

Passion, or hard-headedness, must have made my mother sign up for Spanish II despite her teacher's gift. My mother knew she was wrong.

"In order to get to Spanish II, I had to pass my old teacher, who always stood outside her door before class. She always shook her head slightly and pursed her lips in disappointment."

"But you passed Spanish II, didn't you?"

"No, I flunked it."

Luckily scientists haven't uncovered a Spanish gene.

Being bussed was a blessing in disguise because I got to stretch my wings, get some independence, and create my own little identity. I wouldn't be known as anybody's little sister. I loosened up in Spanish class and found a certain stability at my new school that, after Cory's death, I'd longed for at home. Little did I know my whole world was about to come tumbling down.

To an extent I'd lived in Dawn's shadow. "Dawn has all the personality," praised my mother.

"She has that thick hair that'll look pretty no matter how she wears it," she rubbed in. In fact, Dawn was happy and popular. In contrast to my mother, she always smiled, and I couldn't get enough of her. Even though she was two years older than me, people always thought we were twins, which I thought was ridiculous because she was a couple shades lighter than I was. Her hair was sandy brown while mine was a darker brown. We'd spend hours playing with our paper dolls or playing school. She'd lie on her back, place her big feet on my belly, grab my hands and hoist me up in the air. We'd just giggle. On the night before Thanksgiving one year she put on her pink nightgown, I put on my green one, and we sat on the kitchen floor and played Jacks while the turkey basted and the chitlins filled our apartment with their funky smell.

Apparently Dawn couldn't sit still. She used to turn flips on my mother's bed, and when we went outside, she couldn't resist turning a cartwheel or two. With the insurance money she got after Cory's death, my mother signed her up for gymnastics, and every Wednesday I went along to watch. I still have a picture of her taken right before a show she did to the theme of "Happy Days". She had on a shimmering lime green leotard, a short white poodle skirt and a little white scarf tied around her neck. Her hair was brushed back and she was wearing white earrings. Her most captivating accessories, though, were her thick, luscious eyebrows and her dimples. She was kneeling, her arms were raised, and her long fingers that were almost a carbon copy of mine, waved joyfully. We were sure she'd be the next Olga Korbut.

One night I awoke to my mother frantically shaking my shoulder.

"I can't get Dawn's nose to stop bleeding. She just coughed up a half cup of blood."

Felicia and I got dressed in the middle of the night, and my mother drove us to the emergency room.

"Dawn has aplastic anemia," I'd repeat to my friends, her friends, our family in Toledo or to whom ever else asked about her. Eyes would glaze over and heads would nod stupidly. Knowing they expected more, I explained that her bone marrow had stopped working. As though reading out of my friend's encyclopedia, I'd continue, "She doesn't have any platelets, so when she bleeds she doesn't stop. She gets platelets and blood from other people." I had to repeat this – over and over and over. I was barely twelve years old.

But those words never satisfied me even though "aplastic" and "anemia" would become two of the hardest words in the English language to utter. Even though I said them a lot, the words didn't seem real, not even when I heard them for the first time. They hadn't been directed at me, and by the blank look on my mother's face when the doctor first linked "aplastic" and "anemia" to "your little girl", they hadn't been real to her either. Strangely enough, I also remembered the doctor telling my mother that leukemia would have been easier to treat.

For the first time in my life, I had to have my blood drawn, and I was being terrified of the needle. My mother had told me to be strong because if my blood matched Dawn's, I could give her some of my bone marrow, and maybe she would live. Neither of my parents was compatible, and since Felicia had been from my mother's first marriage, I was her best shot.

Unfortunately, we didn't match, and the next year and a half would be filled with Dawn's blood: nose bleeds, bleeding gums and blood transfusions. Every day after work, my mother would drive thirty minutes home to pick me up and drive thirty minutes back to the hospital just so we could spend a couple hours with her at Riley Children's Hospital. I'd been alone in the hospital one time when her IV had to be changed. She'd asked me to hold her hand because her arms were so bruised and battered from all the needles. I took her hand and turned my head because I couldn't bear to see her crying, knowing that there was nothing I could do to help her. I thought of the times she fought my battles with a few of the neighborhood kids and of the summers we spent together with our father in Toledo. I watched my beloved sister die a slow, painful death just three years after losing my brother. And, like with his death, I hadn't been at the hospital when she'd passed. I'd never gotten the chance to say good-bye or even tell her how much I loved her. When she was alive, I felt like I lived in her shadow. She now lives in the shadows of my childhood.

No one ever talked to Felicia and me about Cory and Dawn's deaths. Not my mother, not my father, not even a therapist. I had been so careful to avoid upsetting my mother, who from then on constantly reminded us that she "couldn't take anything else". Years would pass before I would even mention their names around my mother, who managed to share how relieved she was that Grandma Thelma hadn't lived to see Dawn die, who she'd always had a soft spot for. She'd passed away of complications due to her diabetes shortly after Cory's death.

I had known, even then, that my home situation was not normal. More than that, I'd spent the rest of my childhood feeling like something was wrong with me. I knew I wasn't like everybody else. None of my friends had ever dealt with death. How could I relate to any of them? Michelle was the only person who seemed to understand because she'd been Dawn's friend. She lived in the same apartment complex, and for whatever reason, she befriended me after Dawn's death, and would become one of my dearest, closest friends.

*H*ow I longed to talk to my dear, close friend about what I was going through those first months in Holland. I felt like I was watching another piece of my identity die. I'd been raised to strive to be a strong, independent black woman but found myself even doubting my own blackness. Black women have had to endure much more than what I was going through. My own mother could attest to that. I felt so ashamed for being so weak that I didn't dare share any of this with Michelle or my mother; I was sure they'd be disappointed in me; I know I was.

Still, that image of my mother sitting at her stenograph, when her life was falling apart around her must have given me the courage to keep going. My mother embodied strength and independence and just thinking about her motivated me to stop feeling sorry for myself. When I moved to Holland, I'd left my mother and, symbolically, my childhood behind. I realized that my life was no longer intertwined with my mother's and that I had the right to be happy. I was happy with Vinz, and if that meant saying good-bye to my past and my country, I was willing to do so. At the end of those first hard months in Holland, I finally gave myself permission to say good-bye to Dawn and Cory.

After Christmas and the New Year, Vinz and I spent every weekend looking for a place of our own. Finally, in April 2000, after living in Holland for six months, we bought a flat in Leiden, about fifteen minutes from The Hague. Leiden came into the historic spotlight when, in the sixteenth century, it joined other Dutch cities in a revolt against Spanish rule. Leiden was besieged for months when, in a strategic move, the city's main dike was cut, allowing the city to be flooded. Ships were able to break through the siege with food, supposedly plain white bread and raw fish, for the starving people. In return for its loyalty, Leiden received the gift of a university, which is among the oldest in Europe.

It was the place I needed to be to continue writing my dissertation. And the view from our fifth-floor apartment was splendid. We looked out over a *gracht*, a canal that runs through a city, and delighted in watching rowers from the university glide by. Just like the water in the canal, my life started to flow a bit more evenly. It was June by the time we finished the renovations to our first home and settled in. We'd sold all our furniture in a yard sale before we left New Orleans so we had nothing. Vinz's friends and family donated a chair here and a table there, so we didn't have to invest too much money in decorating.

By that time I'd also gotten a social security card, which meant I could work. Vinz suggested I contact one of the many language schools. Since Dutch isn't widely spoken outside of Holland and its territories in the Caribbean, the Dutch place a high value on learning languages. Historically, in fact, they were some of the world's most efficient merchants and traders so they had to speak the language of the other. That's all interesting to know, but concretely it was perfect for me because I had a skill that was in demand.

One Sunday I was pumped up at the prospect of putting a piece of my life back together. I asked Vinz where I could get the paper and start going through the want ads. He grinned and informed me that papers weren't delivered on Sundays.

"How can there not be a Sunday paper?" I asked in disbelief and disappointment. "Don't Dutch people look in the want ads for jobs?"

"Since pretty much everything is closed on Sunday, that's all in the Saturday paper."

Of course, I hadn't picked up a Saturday paper.

Well, I figured I'd already waited all those months without a job, what was another week? By August 2000 a language school called Linguarama, responded to my resumé. They were looking for ESL-certified teachers to teach business English to professionals. I'd be teaching the language necessary to give presentations, make business calls, write letters and that sort of thing. I didn't have a certificate, but I did have six years' experience teaching Spanish as a second language and several methodology seminars under my belt.

After living in Holland for nearly a year, I was on my way to my job as a freelance language instructor. I wouldn't be teaching at the university level, but I would be working with people from all over the world. I wouldn't be standing in front of a class, but I would be teaching skills to adults who were motivated to progress in their careers by improving their business English. It would be different from what I'd been used to, but then again, everything that year had been different, and I'd come out just fine.

The morning of my first day of work was filled with anticipation. I got my bike from the storage room located in the basement of our apartment building, hopped on and started cycling the ten minutes to the train station. It was a clear morning before 9:00, so I couldn't quite make out the dark mass that was advancing. As it approached, I made out an army of pimple-faced teenagers cycling to school, commandeering the entire bike path as if they owned it. Taken aback, I resisted the primal urge to seek safety on the grass. Who did those teeny-boppers think they were? I was on my side of the bike path, so I wasn't about to back down. I sat up straight on my bike, my face forward in earnest concentration, intent on winning that battle of chicken.

It was to be a one-sided game that I was destined to lose. Those youngsters were too busy chit-chatting to notice my engaging them in a contest of wills. I held my ground with the first line of troops but fell back as the middle ranks stormed by, oblivious to my attempt to hold my ground. What was it about the Dutch, a mild-mannered sort, when they got on their bikes? They failed to obey the basic rules of engagement: they cycled through red lights, made turns without signaling and threatened to run down poor, unsuspecting pedestrians making the mistake of using the crosswalk.

I figured there must be a super-gene embedded in the Dutch constitution because in the year I'd lived in Holland, I'd seen them do things on bikes that made me shudder just to watch. I'd seen women transporting their newborns on their chests wrapped up in cloth carriers and men balancing cases of Heineken. Perhaps the most astounding feat performed on two wheels was a youngster whose left leg had been plastered in a cast from ankle to thigh. She'd been pedaling with one leg, using one arm to steer and the other to secure her crutches under her arm. When I'd seen that performance, I'd wanted to scream, "Hey, lady. Wouldn't it be easier to take the bus that's driving behind you?" But I'd restrained that urge, reminding myself of the bike gene.

The Linguarama Language School was a microcosm of Dutch society insofar as my colleagues, as well as the clientele, had backgrounds as diverse as the languages taught, all by native speakers. The environment was unpretentious because we were all in the same boat, that is, we were all foreigners looking to connect with people outside our intimate circles by broadening our networks. We wanted our skills to remain viable even though teaching business language wasn't our main professional focus. We needed to have a reason to get out of bed and jump on our bikes because we had somewhere to be.

While it still wasn't home, Holland had ceased to be a foreign country to me during that first year. I'd picked up a few words of Dutch, was getting along with Vinz's family and getting to know his friends. I started preferring Holland's international flavor. I loved seeing newspapers from around the world and was even getting used to subtitles. Most of all, to the Dutch and other Europeans I'd met, I wasn't first and foremost black. True, I was a foreigner, but, when strangers found out I was American, they were interested in where I'd come from and why I'd chosen to live in their country. In fact, I was feeling more welcome after one year in Holland than I'd felt during most of my life in America.

Part III

There were two surefire ways to get my friends and family to come check out the new life I'd built in Holland: a funeral or a wedding, and since I wasn't planning on dying anytime soon, I opted for the second. Vinz and I had been together for five years and in Holland for two, and I told myself that I wanted the people who had so trustfully let me go and pursue this new life to meet and mingle with the people who'd so graciously embraced me, not only as Vinz's girlfriend, but as Carolyn – even if I was a bloody American, as I was sometimes referred to.

I was surprised by my urge to marry Vinz, given my parents' track record – both had been married and divorced twice. Although the last time we'd talked about marriage at length we were still in

New Orleans, the subject had popped up from time to time. Vinz would reassure me that he wanted to be married to me. What he didn't want was to be surrounded by people who hadn't been a significant part of our lives but had been invited anyway because we'd felt obligated. "And weddings are so expensive," he'd grumble before reminding me about his former colleague who'd spent $20,000 on his wedding and filed for divorce the following year. "He's still paying for the engagement ring," he'd add just in case I'd forgotten.

I agreed with each of his arguments. Truth be known, I wasn't one of those girls who'd fantasized about the long white dress, the bridesmaids decked out in teal tea dresses and the corny vows we'd made up. I wasn't expecting a ring that cost more than a year's salary at Linguarama. I wasn't even naïve enough to believe that marriage would change our relationship. It was more than that: I'd been craving the stability that I thought could only be satisfied by that particular commitment.

I could've waited for Vinz to get around to proposing, or I could do it myself. And, if I was going to go that far, I figured I'd go with style. To Paris. I had never been to Paris, so why not plan a weekend for two in the world's (arguably) most romantic city? To make the moment more special for Vinz, I'd decided to pop the question in Dutch. Even though his English was almost perfect, I didn't want there to be any misunderstandings at the moment of truth.

I had no idea how to say the words, so what did I do? I went to the bank and asked my account manager for a crash course in the language of popping the question. Angelique was a bubbly blond girl who loved her horse and her motorcycle. She was one of the first people to befriend me after Vinz and I had moved into our new apartment in Leiden. Sometimes I'd invent reasons to go to the bank just so I could have a cup of tea and chat with her. Just as I'd thought she would, she turned out to be a willing conspirator. Not only did she write down what I needed to say and coach my pronunciation, she also suggested a few of her favorite restaurants in Paris. She wasn't as enthusiastic when I detailed the plan.

"I bought a gold engagement band," I explained. "While we're having dinner at a chic restaurant, I'm going to secretly slip it to our waiter and ask him to drop it in Vinz's champagne glass."

I was proud of myself for coming up with that piece of brilliance, but Angelique wasn't as impressed.

"That's so American," she blurted out with a directness that the Dutch are infamous for.

"But I am American," I pointed out.

"Why don't you just ask him?"

"Have you ever asked anyone to marry you?"

She thought about it for a few seconds and laughed. "That's a good point."

A couple weeks later, Vinz and I jumped into our blue Volkswagen Golf and turned right towards gay Par-ee. As we made our way west through Holland, I felt just as excited as I had when I was in college and my roommates and I would go on a road trip. Except now I was driving with my man instead of driving somewhere in hopes of finding one. Instead of traveling through states like Indiana and Ohio, I was following signs in Dutch, Flemish and French telling me which highways went to cities like Brussels, Luik and Paris.

I started daydreaming about our destination and its people. America's stock portrayal of a Parisian was the intense little man sporting a thin mustache and black beret, strolling along the boulevard with a freshly baked, crusty baguette peeking through the crook of his arm. Luckily, I had other images to fall back on. I'd learned that Paris had been good to black writers like James Baldwin, Richard Wright and Chester Himes, the father of the black detective novel. Paris claimed them when America had cast them off as illegitimate offspring. Josephine Baker and Nina Simone, for example, had found refuge from American racism as well as an appreciative audience for their art. In the end, they'd found bits of themselves during their stints in this captivating city.

Josephine Baker had risen above her banana dance and took on an impressive role as part of the French resistance during the Second World War. She'd walked the talk of diversity before it had become the fashionable corporate buzzword of the 1990s. While living in France, she'd also adopted more than ten children of all different races, ethnicities and religions to prove that diversity could beget harmony.

I was about to make the city my own. Paris was going to backdrop the engagement story that I would joyfully tell my children's children. From the passenger's seat of our car, I peeked at Vinz, a sly grin adorning my face, knowing he didn't suspect a thing. I was mentally patting myself on the back when his sudden, "What's up? Why are smiling like that?" dragged me out of my reverie.

"Oh, nothing. I'm just curious about Paris."

After a short five-hour drive, we pulled into the City of Lights. To get to our hotel, we had to drive around the Arc du Triomphe, the mother of all roundabouts. A veritable Bermuda Triangle, cars must have disappeared in this whirlpool where there are no driving lanes, no stoplights and no conspicuous right of way. It freaked me out, so we were lucky I wasn't driving. Vinz, on the other hand, had a smirk on his lips and a gleam in his eye. When he bogarded his way onto the circle, he reminded me of a mad scientist cackling and rubbing his hands together in sinister anticipation. I clutched the door handle and pressed my right foot firmly into the mat, willing Vinz to heed incoming traffic as he exited onto our street.

We checked into the Hotel Caroline and spent the afternoon climbing the Eiffel Tower, admiring Notre Dame and promising to actually go inside the Louvre the next time we were in town. What can I say about this fascinating city that hasn't already been captured in words, images, song and mime except this: what really made an impression on me was a street market. Nor was it just any street market – it was a

Parisian street market with quaint awnings sheltering bright, colorful food. Tray upon tray of cheeses decorated one stand, while next to it plump grapes and other luscious fruits begged to accompany their neighbor on any beautifully arranged platter. Who knew that fish could be displayed with such an artistic eye that even someone like me, who didn't even like fish, was on the verge of buying one? Everything had been presented as though a passer-by were the guest of honor at an intimate dinner party. I got the impression that Parisians didn't just go to the market, they experienced it. I'd heard more than one European accuse the French of arrogance. After my first day in Paris, I concluded that the French had every reason to be as arrogant as they wanted to be.

That night we decided to go barhopping after dinner. Our first stop was an Irish pub. Right after ordering our drinks, Vinz excused himself to take advantage of the facilities. I waited until he was out of sight before taking the small box out of my coat pocket. I opened it and took out the ring. I looked at the plain gold band, way too big for my thumb, and wondered if I was crazy. I was about to defy all convention, like the so-called broads in the movies of the 30s and 40s, and within twenty-four hours propose to a man. Wondering what his reaction would be, my hands trembled slightly, and I almost dropped the ring. Just in the nick of time, I saw him walking toward the bar where I'd been sipping my glass of wine and hastily dropped the box and the ring back in my coat pocket before he saw them.

"Ready to get out of here?" he asked as he gulped down the last of his beer.

We walked through the Latin Quarter, which was hopping that Saturday evening in October. As we strolled down the street, we saw waiters standing outside bistros yelling out that evening's specialty. I reached in my pocket and grabbed the ring to remind me of my purpose. Every light in every building seemed to be blaring in my face. Tourists like us walked arm in arm, heads jerking left then right so as not to miss anything. I toyed with the ring in my pocket, pulling it on and off my finger. I could hardly think of anything other than what I'd been planning to do the next evening. Did I really have the guts to propose? As if to reassure my unspoken doubt, Vinz took my hand in his. What if he said "no"? Would I have to break up with him? Should I move out of our apartment? What was the etiquette for a rejected marriage proposal?

As we'd come close to the end of the Latin Quarter, I'd come close to chickening out of my plan. I freed my hand from Vinz's soft, warm grip and slipped it into my pocket, needing to feel the cool, smooth symbol of my future. Too bad I'd only had one glass of wine. I could have used a shot of Dutch courage right then. *Where's the ring?* I thought. I felt around my pocket again. No ring. I checked my other pocket. No ring. "Shit!" I whispered to myself.

I saw Vinz's lips moving, but for the life of me I had no clue what he'd been saying to me. Feigning attention, I just nodded my head and muttered, "Uh huh". I dug into my jeans' pockets. It had to be there.

Nope. No ring.

By then Vinz must have sensed my growing panic because he looked down at me and asked, "What's up, baby?"

"Nothing," I said weakly, searching my coat pockets one more time in case the wizard who'd made it disappear had had his laugh and put it back where it belonged. I couldn't believe it. It must have dropped out when Vinz grabbed my hand. How was I going to propose now? I couldn't just come out and ask him to marry me without any theatrics to distract him.

"Girrrrl, it's now or never; jump to it!"

urged that voice inside me that I'd come to liken to the Yoruban god Eleggua, known to stand at the crossroads of life, often resorting to trickery to teach the valuable lessons of life. Like Eleggua, my inner voice wasn't always politically correct, but I was learning to trust my teeth-suckin', neck-twistin', "I'ma-tell-you-like-it-is" instinct because it always did good by me.

"This is the Seine, isn't it?" I asked Vinz casually.

"The one and only," he replied.

So I stopped suddenly and took a deep breath. Plan B actually had a romantic appeal because Vinz loved the water. *"Now or never, girl."*

"Wanna know why I planned this weekend in Paris?" I asked, my heartbeat sounding as loud as the lapping water.

He nodded.

Did he suspect anything?

"You remember a couple minutes ago when you asked me if something was wrong?"

"Yeah," he said, stopping.

"Well, I was panicking because I'd lost the ring."

"What ring?" he said, the puzzled frown on his forehead giving way to a knowing grin on his lips.

"I brought you here to Paris to propose."

I looked up at him and he was *smiling*. Before I lost my nerve, I grabbed his hand and said, in my best Dutch, "*wil je met me trouwen?*"

Without the slightest hesitation he said, "Ja, natuurlijk." And we became engaged.

I beamed an excited smile and threw my arms around his neck. We kissed. I did the Cabbage Patch – well, in my head. Paris has meant so many things to so many people, but for me, it'll always be known as the city where my gold engagement ring is lying in some gutter waiting for me to find it.

On the drive back a couple days later, I had plenty of time to reflect on what I'd just gotten myself into. Now that the deed was done, and I'd gotten what I wanted, I admitted to myself that maybe, just maybe, marrying this man meant more to me than fusing our pasts and our worlds and feeling stable in my new life. Deep down I was testing this white man to see just how far he was willing to go with a black woman. I needed to prove that my interracial relationship meant more to him than having great sex with an exotic woman.

As with all things, America had racialized love long before I'd ever taken the headlong plunge. The white community, spearheaded by Hollywood, had made it clear that, for all intents and purposes, black women were not worthy relationship material. During the 70s and 80s, when I was growing up, if we appeared in "white" movies at all, we weren't depicted as healthy, monogamous, loving partners. We were cast as prostitutes or drug addicts. In the last few decades, this has changed but not nearly enough. Even my girl Halle Berry can't get membership to the exclusive romantic comedy club. *Monster's Ball*, for which Berry won an Oscar, has been the only dramatic love story involving a black woman and a white man legitimized by the industry. Other than that one film, black women have continued to be cast as asexual, matronly types like Dr. Baily on *Grey's Anatomy*. In either depiction, black women have stood outside of a good, healthy romantic relationship.

The black community wasn't any better about legitimizing a relationship like mine. I'd heard the old saying that a white man would never want a black woman for anything other than a piece of her round ass. He'd surely never think enough of a black woman to marry one. If that failed to keep black women out of enemy arms, the old "sell-out" argument would. Black men have long been depicted as victims: of the system, of the man, of the hard, black woman whose bad attitude has pushed him into the arms of white and Asian women. She betrayed the race when she failed to support her "good black man" through his prison sentence or drug addiction. She convinced herself that she had to accept his multiple baby mamas.

I never dared tell anyone, not even my closest friends, that I'd preferred white men. I'd been ashamed to admit that I found white men attractive. Had I also racialized love? I'd told myself that I also preferred a man who had big dreams, who'd seen something of the world, and, most of all, who was educated enough to think beyond the black and white thing. But hadn't it been possible to find those things in a black man? Was I really a sell-out? No wonder I'd felt intimidated by the threatening looks of some black men.

I shifted uncomfortably in the front seat as I remembered one evening in DC when a threat from one black man had become palpable. And I hadn't even been dating a white man. I'd been rollerblading through DuPont Circle with my crew of gay boyfriends. We were a motley crew of about five white boys of all sizes and ages, from all walks of life, and brown-skinned, curly-headed me.

We'd been sitting on the fountain steps in DuPont Circle, taking a short break, talking, laughing and having a good time together. We were putting on our wrist guards and helmets, buckling up our skates when a black homeless man walked toward us. He looked at my skating buddies before looking at me and then again at my buddies as they skated off. At that point I hadn't felt worried or scared. In fact, I'd always felt comfortable in DuPont Circle, which had been known as the gay part of DC. But then that man did something peculiar. He raised his right hand, which had taken on the shape of a handgun and pointed it at my head. He pulled the trigger.

First it freaked me out; then it pissed me off. Those men had been true friends to me. They'd taken me, a little girl from Indiana, under their collective wing and become my social life for a minute. And here was this man judging me. He'd refused to see further than the idea that a black woman had the nerve to even socialize with white men. But what made him, or any other black man who'd ever given me a dirty look, think that I'd be with him – even socially – if I hadn't been with the white men? And why hadn't he been willing to take them on? He seemed to wait conveniently until they'd skated away. He'd singled me out for punishment for being a sell-out.

Vinz turned off the radio, and I took advantage of the opportunity of being cooped up in the car, driving through Belgium, to let him know once and for all what he was getting himself into by marrying a black American woman.

"Did I ever tell you that people used to think I was a lesbian?" I said as casually as possible, not wanting to let on how much it had hurt my feelings when one of my best friends had told me her mother had asked if I was a lesbian because she'd never seen me with a man.

"Really?" He grimaced. "Cause you used to wear combat boots?"

"How'd you know that?"

"Monika mentioned it to me the last time we were there."

I reminded myself to give her a piece of my mind the next time we talked. But then again, that was typical Monika, who I'd met when I was in second or third grade. She'd just moved to Indiana from Germany, where she'd been living with her German mother and African-American father until they'd divorced. Her father had moved back to America and remarried a black woman. Monika's stepmother's sister had lived in the one-bedroom apartment next door to me, so I played with Monika whenever she came to visit her auntie. Monika had never been the best keeper of secrets. Not that she'd ever revealed my skeletons maliciously. It was more that she'd blurted things out before thinking about it, like telling Vinz that I'd worn combat boots with skirts.

"Actually, I think people doubted my heterosexuality because they'd never seen me with a black man. And since I wasn't with a black man, there must've been something wrong with me."

I stepped up on my soapbox.

"I've always had the feeling that black women in America were given two choices: marry a black man or stay single. In fact, it's rare to see a black woman walking down the street arm in arm with a white man."

"But I've seen a lot of black men with white women," Vinz remarked.

"In the black community, that's OK," I said. "But not the other way around. Sometimes black people make me feel like a sell-out," I confessed.

"What do you mean?"

"Basically, a sell-out is someone who's betrayed their race. Since I'm black, I should be marrying a black man," I said, getting mad at the unfairness of it. "Yeah," I continued, "for some people, a black man could be in jail, unemployed, on drugs or out there making baby after baby and not taking care of them. Who I find attractive and who makes me happy aren't important. The only thing that matters is that I marry within the race."

In fact, I'd dated black men but was not romantically attracted to them. Truth be told, I'd gone out with them because I'd felt I had to. Out of obligation to my race. I'd always told myself and my friends that I was open to dating just about anybody. That color didn't matter to me. But it did. As I came of age, my fear was that I'd end up marrying a black man with good qualities who I wasn't attracted to just because he was black. I'd always been too embarrassed – and scared – to admit that, when it came down to it, I preferred white men. I never considered it a prejudice, but simply a preference.

Nor could I admit that my mother had always warned me against marrying a black man, never mind that she'd married two black men, one of them my father. Unfortunately, she'd projected her bad experiences onto all black men. I'd still been out to please my mother and had been afraid to imagine how she'd look at a black man that I'd brought home to her. Would she ever accept him? Even still, I'd never approached white men or showed interest because I feared their rejection. Nor did I date every white man who showed an interest in me. I had to find him attractive, and he had to treat me with respect.

All those contradictory messages floating around. From the white community, I should stay single, according to the black community I should marry a black man and from my mother it should be a white man, regardless. In that moment I doubted my feelings: was I with Vinz because he was white or because I'd fallen in love with him? Why couldn't I have resolved these issues before asking him to marry me?

My engagement seemed to spawn another relationship in the form of a new job. One of my colleagues at Linguarama had forwarded an email from the University of Utrecht. Its recently established international campus, University College Utrecht, was expanding its tutorial board. They were looking for people with a master's degree who were familiar with the liberal arts system of education. I sent my resume and got an interview. I discovered that I wouldn't be helping struggling students improve their English or math skills. Rather, I'd be advising a group of forty students through their three-year bachelor's program. In a traditional Dutch university, students decide their major and take courses only in that area. I would help students, who'd come from countries around the world, to choose their courses in preparation for a master's degree.

In addition, I would function as a mentor-cum-guidance counselor, helping students negotiate the demands of living on campus. University College was the first of its kind in this regards because Dutch students typically lived at home or had to find housing for themselves. I was hired not only because I could pass on my knowledge of living abroad and of the liberal arts system, but also because of my teaching skills. Shortly after starting my new job as an advisor, I was asked to teach an academic English course. At last, I would be standing in front of a classroom again. That the other tutors held Ph.D.s in linguistics, anthropology, physics and psychology and came from countries like Ireland, Germany and America added to the appeal. The only downside was the ninety-minute commute one way. But at least I'd make enough money to contribute to our living costs.

By this time I'd gotten over the culture shock of my first year in Holland and the settling in of the second year. This third year promised to be more relaxing. I was getting used to the idea of becoming someone's wife, and my days took on a manageable routine. I'd even found a beauty shop in Amsterdam, so my hair was looking all right. I didn't even mind that our social life revolved around Vinz's friends from the hotel school because I was acquainting myself with his friends' partners and familiarizing myself with the subtleties of Dutch relationships.

Toward the end of these three years, we'd begun planning our wedding, so my increase in salary couldn't have come at a better time. We'd set the date for May 2003 because in the three years I'd lived in Holland, I'd learned that the best chance of good weather was early May or August. The other ten months were anyone's guess. We decided to have a May wedding for another practical reason: we needed time to save since we'd be financing our own big day.

The Dutch are a very "cash and carry" people, which means they don't rely on credit. They buy when they can afford, and that had, thank goodness, rubbed off on me. We'd refused to go into debt over a one-day event that was more about the party than putting on airs. We made a budget and came to the conclusion that we'd be able to save around five thousand euros in the eighteen months until our wedding. As weddings go, we realized we'd be limited so we'd have to cut some corners here and there. We both agreed on keeping it a small *gezellig* (or cosy) affair, inviting only our closest friends and family.

Instead of buying a wedding gown, I'd asked my mother-in-law, an accomplished seamstress, if she'd be willing to help me make a dress. Of course she would, but she'd have to enlist the help of her sister-in-law, who had professional dressmaking experience. Although I'd done this to save money, it was one of the most beautiful memories I have of that period. While I didn't do much more than make tea, I got close to my mother-in-law.

I asked my friend Corinne to act as our wedding planner. She'd briefly worked with Vinz at the Jefferson Hotel, although I didn't meet her until she and her Dutch boyfriend came to visit us in New Orleans. She was a Swiss woman who, like me, ended up in Holland. She was a great organizer and was happy to help out. Plus she did it for free.

To keep within our budget, we relied on Dutch tradition to finance our honeymoon. Corinne informed our guests that we'd like to receive cash in lieu of toasters, towels and the other trifles that pass as wedding gifts. At first, I thought it was tacky to ask your guests for money but then Vinz explained that it was a Dutch custom, and who was I to question it?

We were in the full swing of planning our wedding when something very unexpected happened: I got pregnant. For whatever reason, a few months previous to our engagement, we'd decided it was a good time to try to have a baby. I assumed that since I was already thirty-five, I'd been on the pill for almost my entire adult life and since I was in a stressful period in my life, it would take me a couple of years to even get pregnant. So much for sound planning.

We'd just spent the holidays in America, and I assumed I was extra sensitive to jetlag because I was just so tired. It never occurred to me that I might be pregnant until I realized my period was several weeks late. I'd gotten so caught up in the planning that I'd assumed I was just stressed. I went to my doctor, where it was confirmed that I was going to be a pregnant bride. But how could I be pregnant? I hadn't gained any weight, nor had I experienced morning sickness.

How could I find out I was pregnant five months before my wedding? Stunned, I called Vinz and asked him if he preferred being called "papa" or "daddy".

After congratulating each other, I hung up the phone and cried. I was in shock, not because I was pregnant but because, despite having decided to have a baby, I'd never seen myself as a mother. Although I'd never discounted motherhood, it never figured in my plans. Come to think of if, I'd never planned to be married. Since none of the adults in the immediate circle of my childhood was married, I'd taken for granted that I'd be single, too. My impending wedding coupled with this latest news overwhelmed me because I realized how much I'd longed for both.

Physically, I felt fantastic. I was wearing my pregnancy well, if I did say so myself. I basked in the excitement that my colleagues felt for me and was thrilled when finally I put on my first maternity clothes. I was holding up emotionally, although I was tired. I'd had many late nights grading papers and writing lesson plans. We'd also spent quite a few evenings listening to bands playing at various venues. We'd opted for a live band for our reception over a DJ, and before we made a decision, we thought it would be a good idea to see for ourselves how the band interacted with a crowd.

I didn't know if it was exhaustion, hormones or good old-fashioned pre-wedding jitters. Maybe the fact that, one by one, my friends informed me that they wouldn't be able to come to my wedding after I'd moved heaven and earth to attend theirs. Perhaps I'd been down because neither my mother nor father nor sister could manage to come see the life I'd made for myself. Whatever had initiated it, I'd picked an argument with Vinz that blew up into an "I'm-not-speaking-to-him-for-a-couple-of-days" fight. I'd got myself worked up so much, I considered calling off the wedding.

Instead, I was overcome with the urge to call my father. I'd always believed that I hadn't needed him. For all intents and purposes, my mother had raised me. She'd been the one who'd comforted me when I hadn't had a date for the senior prom. She'd pushed me to excel in school, convincing me that I'd had the brains to become a doctor. She'd complimented me on my legs, telling me constantly how shapely they were. She'd also been the one who'd resented my father for not paying child support. In high school when I'd call to talk to him, she'd accompany her disappointment by saying, " I don't understand why you call him. He hasn't done anything to help you. If I were you, I'd leave him alone." When she'd realized I was intent on talking to him, she'd throw in, "Make sure you reverse the charges."

No matter what she'd thought or said, he was my father, and I loved him despite his not sending money and despite my mother's bitter prediction that one day he was going to call me and want a relationship with me. "I hope you hang up on him," she'd exhorted. Ready to walk away from my fiancé, as my mother had walked away from my father, it dawned on me how crucial a father's influence is. How else would a girl or young woman learn how to be intimate with a man if she'd never seen intimacy at home? If her father didn't explain that men communicate differently than women, who would she learn that from? Couples had fights, but that didn't mean they were destined to split up. I'd never learned that.

Unfortunately, my father had been away far more than he'd been around. I'd never admitted to my mother how sad I felt that my father had rarely called me just to ask how I was doing. I'd never let on to her that I'd internalized that fact and assumed that there had been something wrong with me. Why else wouldn't he call? Instead, I'd defended his phantom presence. Through my teens and young adult years, six months could go by without so much as a word from him. I would blame myself for his inability to cherish me like I always imagined a father should.

'Was I not pretty or smart enough? What was it about me that was so unlovable?

Cliff Huxtable adored his daughters. When *The Cosby Show* broke out in the eighties I ached all over for a father who was present – physically and emotionally – and involved in his kids' lives, not to mention a father who was a doctor and had money. They say a girl chooses a man just like her father, and if I never believed it before, I did while I was dialing his number and waiting for him to answer. My intended was tall and evenly proportioned just like my father. They're both laid back and would rather try to make me laugh than argue. On the flip side, they had no problem putting me in my place when I'd gone too far. They both had the ability to make me doubt myself.

Just months before my wedding, I was calling my father to ask him the same questions I'd never dared to ask when I was younger.

"Hey, Dad," I said somewhat despondently when he picked up the phone.

"What's the matter with you?" he asked in that playful tone that made my eyes well up with tears.

Out poured my anxiety over this life-changing event, my exhaustion, my fears about becoming a parent and, most of all, my insecurity. It all came out in the one question that would change my relationship with the most important man in my life up to that point.

"What's wrong with me?"

"Why do you assume there's something wrong with you?"

Silence.

"Let me tell you something, Little Carolyn. You make me so proud. I know I haven't always been the best father, but I've always loved you. There's nothing wrong with you. If Vinz doesn't see what I see, then maybe you shouldn't get married."

In that one telephone call, I got the validation from my father that I'd longed for. He told me how proud of me he was. He told me how smart I was and that he'd always trusted my judgement. It had taken me thirty-six years to actually believe those words, when I was symbolically leaving his house to go to my future husband's. Almost as an afterthought, he added, "Why don't you come and stay with me in Toledo for a few weeks; make Vinz come and get you?"

I didn't leave Vinz, but I did leave behind a childish ideal of who my father should be. As our wedding day approached, I understood that Cliff Huxtable could only exist in a made-up world where fathers always said and did the right thing by their daughters. I was learning to accept and respect my father's clay feet instead of trying to gild them for display. More importantly, after so many years, I finally had a reply to my mother's asking me why I called him. Because whenever I called Dad he was there for me, and no matter what my situation was, he understood me and somehow found the magic words to make me feel better and help me. If he wasn't there when I called, he always called me back. With all the love and forgiveness I could muster, I put him on his pedestal, clay feet and all.

Neither of my parents would end up coming to my wedding, which I managed to accept with a measure of aplomb. As I sat there in Leiden's City Hall before the Justice of the Peace, Mr. Pancake, as he performed the ceremony (much of which I didn't follow because it was done in … well … Dutch), I couldn't help but imagine turning around and seeing my father sitting next to my in-laws, his long arms dangling about like Pinocchio's, smiling despite the perpetual cigarette somehow hanging on the lips that were a carbon copy of mine.

That image of him has stayed with me my entire adult life, even though it was one of the earliest childhood memories I have of him. I'd spent many a summer and Christmas vacation in Toledo with him, my grandmother Elizabeth, his nine brothers and sisters and all my cousins. I'd get off the Greyhound bus and look around anxiously for him. I'd crack a smile of utter joy to see him coming to pick me up.

Only this time I was imagining that he had come to Holland to give me away. Centuries-old marble floors replaced the grubby linoleum at the Greyhound bus station; Dutch masterpieces now lined the walls in place of signs indicating gate numbers and departure times. And I'm kissing Vinz's lips after saying "*Ja, ik wil*," instead of pecking my father's lips and hugging him tightly. Vinz and I are holding hands, newlyweds, walking into the elegant main hall to the receiving line as the memory of my hands entwined with my father's, swinging as we left the bus station, faded to the background of my mind.

When Vinz had asked me where I wanted to go on our honeymoon, I replied, "Cuba," without a second's hesitation. I'd fallen in love with Cuban literature during graduate school and had dreamed of experiencing its culture firsthand. Because I was six months pregnant by the time we'd said our vows, we decided to keep things low-key. We went to a travel agent and booked the "fly and drive" package. As well as hotel accommodations throughout Cuba, we'd be equipped with a road map and the keys to a Jeep. The rest was up to us.

Our plane landed after midnight in Oriente where a young and visionary Fidel Castro had landed his yacht, the *Granma,* in a move that would result in the Cuban Revolution. A bus had been waiting to drive us from the airport to our hotel. By the time our luggage got loaded and we dragged ourselves on board and sat down, I could barely keep my eyes open. Showing the bus driver my passport was the last thing I remembered doing before falling into a deep sleep.

A couple hours later the bus stopped. We gathered up our luggage, stumbled off the bus and went inside the hotel. Vinz walked over to the reception desk and checked in. I sat in a nearby chair and closed my weary eyes.

"Where's your passport?" he asked from across the hall.

I reached inside my purse. I didn't feel it. In a huff, I started taking everything out.

"Where's my passport?" I grumbled to myself.

It wasn't in my purse, so I grabbed my backpack.

No passport.

"Vinz, can you bring me my suitcase please?"

"Take the clothes out," he suggested after I'd opened it. Irritated, I treated him to an I'm-not-stupid look.

No passport.

"But you had it on the bus, right? You showed it to the driver," he reminded me as we were stuffing the clothes back in.

Oh. My. God. Somebody must have ripped it off me while I was asleep. My hands were trembling as the enormity of the situation swept over me. I was an American citizen in Cuba illegally. With no proof of my identity. There was no American embassy to assist me with a replacement passport. If I contacted the authorities in America, I'd be fined thousands of dollars on top of going through the ordeal.

As the kind lady behind the front desk picked up the phone to contact the bus driver, I just *knew* it was an exercise in futility. What were the chances that he'd find my passport? Lo and behold, the driver found it on our seat. It had been so dark on the bus, and I'd been so sleepy, I hadn't realized that I'd not slipped it in my purse. What's more, he arranged for a cab to drive my passport back to me. I couldn't believe I'd found my passport, which must have been considered a high commodity in some circles. I didn't even want to imagine what could have happened had it fallen into the wrong hands. Visions of Vinz having to leave the country while I stayed and gave birth to our first child in some musty old prison left a bad taste in my mouth. Perhaps more than that, I couldn't believe the honesty and the good will of three people who went out of their way to help me. It set the pace for our honeymoon.

The next few days we recovered from our jetlag and explored Santiago de Cuba, birthplace of the nineteenth-century mulatto general Antonio Maceo, whose feats during Cuba's wars for independence continue to be commemorated throughout the island. We drove up to the Castillo del Morro, the best preserved Spanish castle, and were astounded by its beauty. Built on a cliff, the castle overlooked a bay, which was flanked on both sides by lush vegetation. I felt like the daughter of some seventeenth-century aristocrat who spent hours looking over the horizon for any sign of her lover's ship, returning after months abroad. Vinz, of course, imagined spotting the famous ghost ship, the *Flying Dutchman*. I understood why, in its heyday, colonial Cuba had been dubbed the pearl of the Caribbean. It had to be the most beautiful place on earth.

We left Oriente and drove west. Vinz had insisted on driving through the Sierra Maestra, seeing as we had a Jeep and plenty of time. Unfortunately, Cuba's poverty was most remarkable there, off the beaten path. Still, taking that route rendered a portrait of Cuba we'd never have seen otherwise. Its crumbled infrastructure was most visible in public transportation. Indeed, according to our trusty *Lonely Planet* guidebook, "lifters' were commonplace. It was not gratuitous hitchhiking but a bona fide means of transportation, like cycling was in Holland. Groups of people would hang out along the roadways for hours if necessary, waiting for a ride to wherever they needed to go. They'd wave *pesetas* and dollars to every passing vehicle – cars, buses, motorcycles and ox-pulled wagons. Anything that would get them to their destination.

Ignoring my mother's warnings to never pick up strangers, Vinz and I picked up various lifters, from an American Jehovah's Witness spreading the Word, to a young woman needing to get to Camagüey to visit her small kids, to a husband transporting his sick wife to the hospital. My Spanish came in handy. I'd been able talk to the people in their language, which had turned out to be the best way to get to know the country and the people.

Apart from its politics and extreme poverty, Cuba had one thing in common with America: its culture, society, politics and history had all been built on the foundation of slavery. Historically, blacks in Cuba and America had dealt with similar issues, particularly the relationship between skin color, hair grade and their place in the socio-cultural hierarchy. I'd never once thought I'd get to go to Cuba considering the restrictive and ridiculous US politics and policies toward the island. For a long time I was content with getting to know the colorful culture through its vibrant and oh-so-rich-literature, which resonates as melodiously as its music.

Perhaps that was the reason I'd been captivated by *Cecilia Valdés o la Loma del Angel*, a nineteenth-century Cuban novel that was to be the focal point of my dissertation. Although its white, intellectual male author had appropriated the black female body to decry slavery and show how its nefarious influence permeated every institution on the island, the novel reflected modern-day America. *Cecilia Valdés* was to be read as a realistic portrait depicting the futility of Cuba's extant social hierarchy, which pitted Spanish-born against Creole, tobacco against sugar cane planters, light-skinned blacks against darker-skinned ones as well as depicting the inhumanity of slavery, all of which were toxic for an emerging Cuban national identity. The black female body would be hailed as the quintessential symbol of what it meant to be Cuban: a mixed whole that transcended its various parts.

Cecilia Valdés was the result of an illegitimate relationship between a lower-class mulatto woman and her white, married lover, a powerful landowner and slave trader. Cecilia ultimately became entangled in a deadly love triangle, pursued by a poor musician, Jose Dolores Pimienta, whom she scorned because of his blackness. She submitted to the affections of Leonardo, who ended up being her half-brother. Rather than legitimize their relationship, Leonardo left Cecilia and become engaged to Isabela Ilincheta, heiress to a large tobacco plantation. A pregnant Cecilia discovered Leonardo's betrayal and enlisted Pimienta to extract her revenge. He killed Leonardo on his wedding day. Cecilia was sent to jail, where her daughter would be born outside the legitimacy of marriage, destined to perpetuate the vicious circle.

Issues like passing, the inferior status of dark-skinned black people, the illegitimacy of black families, good hair vs. bad hair and so on emerged in that novel. Ironically, I'd grown up feeling the sting of those very issues, and reading *Cecilia Valdés* showed me that they were nothing more than the remnants of an economic system whose supporters were so desperate to sustain it that they resorted to degrading the essence of an entire people as their justification. One of the system's main sources of power continued to be the internalization of stereotypes and untruths on the part of blacks and whites. I refused to continue to buy into those issues.

For me, visiting Cuba was like going to a family reunion: I didn't know half the people there, but I knew we were related. What's more, with each passing day, I'd come to notice that most of the Cubans actually looked like me. Why had it taken me so long to notice the lack of big, blond-haired, blue-eyed white people? For the first time since I'd met Vinz, *he* was the minority. When I spoke Spanish with the locals, they thought I was Cuban, and no amount of explaining could convince them that I *wasn't* a second or third-generation Cuban living in Miami.

Even the police mistook me for one of their own. We were a couple hours outside of Havana when two officers waved us down and pulled us over.

"Oh, shit," I spat as Vinz slowed down. "What if they ask to see my passport?"

"Just relax, Carolyn," he tried to reassure me. "Let's see what they want."

Turns out they wanted a lift. Who were we to turn down the police, especially the Cuban police? They got in the back and closed the doors. Once we got back on the road, they started chatting to me. How'd they know I spoke Spanish? So, we started talking about lots of things – Fidel Castro was not one of them – and somehow the conversation veered towards American tourists. I mentioned how relieved I'd been that I'd felt no hostility because I was American.

The two policemen looked at each other, and one said, obviously perturbed, "*No eres Cubana?*" After assuring them that I was 100% American, they apologized profusely for hailing us down, explaining that they did so only because they thought I was one of them. I couldn't be mad; on the contrary, I was touched because Cuba had actually claimed me as one of its own, something America had never done.

After that Vinz and I agreed to take a break from picking up lifters. Anyway, we were to be spending the following five days in Havana and wouldn't be driving as much. Havana was a skeleton of its previous splendor. Despite the faded, peeling pastels painted on baroque-styled colonial architecture, it still whispered its beauty into the ear of whomever was alert enough to hear. Having been to Mexico and Puerto Rico, I wasn't naïve about the poverty. But nothing had prepared me for the pride Cubans had in themselves and in their country.

I felt safe strolling about the country's capital city despite the visibly armed military guarding the streets. No one was interested in stealing anything we had. It would have been beneath them to rob us of the fancy 35mm camera that Vinz toted around. Random people would strike up conversation, giving us all sorts of (sometimes false) information about the city's history. Locals were more than happy to give us directions to this restaurant or that museum. The only thing they expected in return was one dollar. Even for unsolicited services, they'd expect a one-dollar tip. One morning we'd left our hotel and headed towards the parking lot. As we approached the Jeep, we noticed a man stand up and start spraying window cleaner on the windshield. We thought it was part of the hotel service until he asked for a tip. He was there the next morning, bright and early, waiting for us.

We took it all in stride, although it was humbling to realize that, as soon as the locals figured out we were tourists, they weren't interested in us, only in our money. And who could blame them? How often did tourists actually see the locals of the country they visited? Didn't locals become faceless, lifeless beings there to make sure tourists got served with a smile? As usual, Vinz managed to see the humor and compared the city to a giant dollar store.

One thing about Havana that turned me off was the fact that locals were not allowed inside the tourist attractions. More than once, I'd witnessed a policeman approach a local and escort him/her away from the entrance to a museum. It was explained to me that Cubans with means had been exempted from this unwritten law. But of course these things were never quite as clear-cut as they seemed because those with the least amount of money tended to be those with the most black blood. In that respect, too, Cuba wasn't that different from America.

As all things must come to an end, the time came for us to leave. At the airport Vinz cruised through customs. They just didn't want to let me go. I got stopped.

"*Eres de los Estados Unidos?*" asked the first customs officer, his voice full of skepticism that I was actually American. By that time, I knew better than to respond in Spanish.

"I'm sorry?" I said, cocking my ear as if to better hear the question.

He'd asked again if I was from the US, to which I replied, "Yes, sir. I am." He looked at my passport and told me to wait just a moment. He called over his colleague who studied my passport in between glances at my face, making sure the two matched.

"You live now in Holland?"

"Yes, I do. Almost four years now."

And then she asked me to wait a moment while she walked away … with my passport. By that time Vinz realized I wasn't walking behind him and walked back to where I stood "waiting a moment". All together those moments added up to about ten minutes, during which I was sure Fidel Castro himself was going to be wheeled out of his sick bed to personally oversee my incarceration for passport fraud and trying to escape the country. My eyes widened and I looked at Vinz for reassurance. What if I never saw him again? What if he never saw his baby? What if I ended up on a raft with the words "Holland or Bust" painted on the handmade sail?

The customs officer handing me back my passport interrupted my desperate reverie.

"Have a good flight to Holland," she said in English, still suspicious of me.

As much as I loved honeymooning in Cuba for those two weeks, I longed to be back in Holland, where all that separated me from motherhood was the rest of the summer. We boarded the plane and settled down in our seats. We had our meal and were ready to watch the movie, which held no interest whatsoever. I had the rest of the flight to think about my parenting strategy.

I'd always believed there was a difference in how black and white people raised their kids. My contemporaries and I grew up believing that white kids disrespected their parents by talking back and calling them names to their faces. In our opinion white kids were spoiled and usually got away with murder (sometimes literally).

Even before I ever decided to become a parent, I decided this: no child of mine was going to run my house or disrespect me. My motto was, "As long as I'm paying the bills, I'm making the rules." When it got time for them to start making the rules, it was time for them to get their own house. And to have a child of mine call me out of my name? To my face? Oh, hell no.

I was raised by a single mother who'd made it clear just how far we could go. I only had to think about saying no to her and I'd get popped. Once I looked at my mother the wrong way, and she told me if I ever did that again she'd knock the shit out of me. And I knew she would, too. I was up in the mirror everyday for a long time making sure I wasn't wearing that look, whatever it was.

I sneaked a peek at Vinz, sitting next to me, absorbed in the movie, and I wondered just how race-based parenting really was. Having seen him interacting with his young nephews, I had the feeling he wouldn't take no shit, either. But still.

My mother had had to be strict (read: mean).

She'd had to work all day. She couldn't afford a nanny or even a babysitter, for that matter. From a young age, my sisters and I had been on our own after school, so my mother had to make sure that our apartment didn't burn down while she was at work. We hadn't even been allowed to turn on her new color TV set until she came home. After work oh girl would touch the screen to see if it was warm. She did not make empty threats and had no problem whooping us, so we thought twice before going against her. I respected my mother, but I also feared her. But did the two necessarily go hand in hand? I wondered if hers had been *black* parenting or necessity parenting?

I knew I'd never lay a hand on my child in anger. Was my only other option to put my child in "time-out" like the white people did? Once again race had penetrated something as intimate as parenting and had me doubting how I'd go about teaching and disciplining my own. And I was scared because I'd be raising biracial children, which I'd always thought was the exclusive domain of white women. Not only that, my children would also be bilingual and bicultural. I would be parenting abroad, away from other blacks. I didn't have anyone that I could go to for advice on how to instill a sense of pride into my child about her heritage since usually black women didn't marry outside the race and certainly didn't live outside the country. What was I getting myself into?

I knew I'd never instill the same rhetoric about race that my mother had instilled in me, but at the same time, I knew I'd been carrying around all that baggage that I'd just begun to unpack and sort through since I'd been in Holland. Still, I didn't know exactly what I'd do save teach my child to embrace all parts of herself, the black, the white, and the mixed, without emphasis on physical beauty according to the ideals of an obsolete black or white aesthetic.

I knew I'd never make my child choose between one or the other or impose a choice on her by labeling her black, as the black community did. By doing that, I'd be denying her her father's heritage. But was it possible to raise a mixed child without mixing her up about who she was?

In America white society would accept my child, depending on her ability to pass, as long as she never touted her blackness. The black community would simultaneously demand my child's loyalty to the race and then ostracize her for being too light-skinned to really understand the authentic black experience. How much better would I fare in Holland?

I knew racism was alive and well and didn't plan on burying my head in the sand about it. That would be foolish. Nor would I prepare my kid for the "inevitable" racist encounters. If I did that I'd have to prepare her for the"inevitable" you're-not-American-enough attacks, or the your-mother-is-a-foreigner comments, or the your-father-is-a-white-racist reactions. So instead of teaching my kid to find as much enjoyment out of life as possible, I'd be teaching her to be anxious, and I refused to do that.

If there was one thing I'd learned during the nearly four years I'd been living in Holland, it was that the Dutch looked further than my biology. The limiting stereotypes attached to being black and female weren't there. For the first time in my life, I'd been able to focus on things other than skin color, like the feats Dutch people could perform on their bikes. When the pilot announced our initial descent into Amsterdam's Schiphol airport, I'd resolved that living in Holland would give me the upper hand in raising a self-confident, self-possessed child.

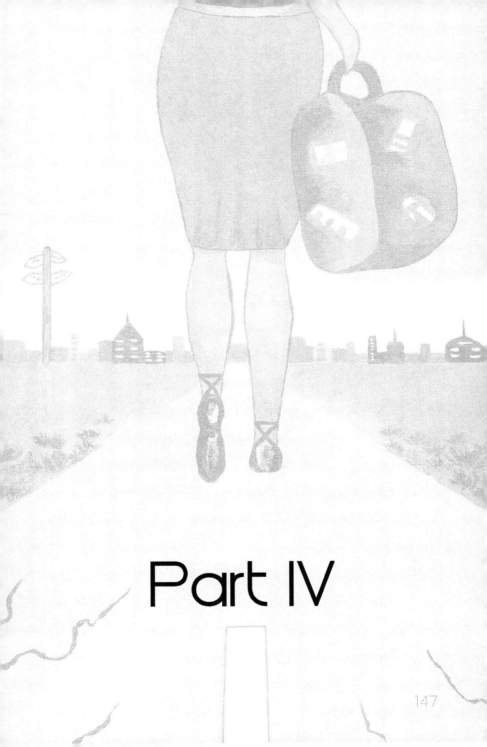

Part IV

"Breathe with me, Carolyn . . . look at me," urged Vinz.

I looked into his concerned blue eyes and somehow managed to summon up the strength just to breathe. I made it through another contraction.

"Now, remember your yoga breathing, Carolyn," Vinz soothed. "Close your eyes and imagine doing your yoga . . . relax . . . keep breathing."

I breathed. I relaxed. For a whole minute. Miraculously, it was enough time to ponder the first of the never-ending contradictions that motherhood would bring. How was it possible that one measly minute could feel like an hour? The next gut-ripping contraction had me silently cussing out motherhood for already bringing so much pain. Another contradiction popped up. Why was I suffering through the torture of natural childbirth when I'd always been a wimp where pain was concerned? Oh yeah, I was too afraid of needles to even consider an epidural. The only thing that helped me through the agony of another contraction was controlled breathing, relaxing and focusing on Vinz's receding hairline – and lovely eyes, of course. Thank goodness it only lasted a minute.

I hadn't counted on the contractions hurting so much that I thought the midwife had started yanking out my innards, one by one. I screamed, and I screamed deeply from the pit of my stomach, just like they do in the movies.

"Carolyn," she said calmly after the excision, her hands gently pressing my belly. "Scream if you want to, but it doesn't help." She was a buxom woman with rosy cheeks, blue eyes and blond ringlets who was about my age, although she looked much older. "Screaming uses a lot of energy. You can better save that energy for pushing out the baby," she informed me in that matter-of-fact manner that Dutch women have.

"*Oh no she didn't,*" sassed the little voice in my head. "*I know she didn't just tell you you couldn't holler. Who does this white wom....*"

Another contraction. I opened my mouth wide, ready to push out a scream that would set off every alarm in our apartment building. But common sense – and exhaustion – had taken over. I breathed through the contraction and discovered that that white woman knew what she was talking about.

"Carolyn, let go of my hand," instructed Vinz. "I gotta pee like a racehorse," he whispered to me, trying to be funny.

Me and my voice just looked at him. "You've got one minute," we said simultaneously.

He made it back, just in time, to see his baby girl, Chloë Dawn Elizabeth, being born two hours shy of my thirty-sixth birthday. He cut the umbilical cord and leaned over and kissed me on the forehead. Then, after being by my side for the entire twenty-one hours of labor and delivery, Vinz left our bedroom and came back with a glass of whiskey. It might have even been a double. He took Chloë in his arms, sat on his side of the bed and just looked at her, smiling.

By this time the *kraamhulp* had arrived. She was a trained nursemaid who would be coming every morning for the next week to show me how to take Chloë's temperature, bathe her and nurse her comfortably. She would also do light housekeeping, make lunch for me and prepare a dish that I could pop in the oven come dinnertime. In Holland it was standard post-natal healthcare and a blessing to this new mother.

"Are you steady enough to take a shower?" she asked about forty-five minutes after I'd given birth. I was grateful that I'd opened myself up to having my baby at home, a custom that the majority of Dutch women still follow. When my mother-in-law had informed me that all three of her children had been born at home, I thought she was crazy … or a hippie. But at that moment, I understood its allure. There were no doctors invading my body with their needles, no sterile hospital smell. I was surrounded by my own stuff. I could shower in my own bathroom, fewer than ten paces from my bedroom. The *kraamhulp* turned on the shower for me and helped me slide my shirt over my head. She put down the toilet lid and sat down, waiting to make sure I didn't keel over.

Relief washed over my entire body as the warm water gushed from the shower head. "*Go 'head girl*," my voice congratulated me for making it through childbirth. "*You go girl*," she continued, and I could just see her nodding her head, dragging down the sides of her mouth and raising her eyebrows in a gesture of being sincerely impressed that I'd had my first child the Dutch way: in my own bed, with a midwife and my husband at my side.

I turned off the shower but didn't manage to turn off my thoughts. I stepped out of the shower and patted myself on the back for making the mother of all commitments. There was no turning back. Sure, I'd made a commitment to building a new life in Holland. Sure, I'd recently made a commitment to my relationship with Vinz. But this was something else. I'd come so far in my life that I'd actually created another life. I padded back to my bedroom, the *kraamhulp* not more than a couple steps behind, and put on my pajamas.

I sneaked a peak at Chloë, who was already sleeping sweetly in her bassinette. Vinz had been dozing off, but when I climbed into bed, he sat upright and kissed me gently on the mouth.

"*Gefeliciteerd met je dochter*," he mumbled, his voice thick with emotion and sleep.

"Congratulations yourself," I replied, snuggling under the covers. The midwife popped her head into the open bedroom door to tell us that she and the *kraamhulp* were leaving and to wish us a good night.

She'd be back promptly at nine the next morning. I looked at the clock and was surprised that it was already 1:00 am. I heard the front door shut quietly as they let themselves out. The adrenaline that had been working overtime up until that point started wearing off. I lay in bed wondering what motherhood had in store for me. I eventually slipped into a satisfied sleep never suspecting that the very next day, motherhood would test me in the most unexpected way.

I'd called my mother to introduce her to her first and only grandbaby. I couldn't wait to share my experience and listen to her first words of advice. I would, unfortunately, have to wait for that. My sister answered my mother's phone and told me that Mom had been admitted to the hospital.

"Is she gonna be okay?"

"They're talking about taking out her gall bladder, so you better call her."

When I got hold of her, my mother was understandably down. She'd been in a lot of abdominal pain and had gone to the emergency room. She was alone in the hospital facing surgery. I tried to lift her spirits by telling her about her first grandbaby, but it didn't work. As usually happened when my mother was feeling down – for whatever reason – I felt my mood changing, too.

"I want to fax you a picture of Chloë. Do you think you could ask a nurse for the fax number?"

She couldn't.

I had a dozing Chloë in one arm and used the other shoulder to hold the phone to my ear while I redialed the hospital's information desk and asked for the nurse's station. I scrambled around for a pen and paper, hoping all the jiggling wouldn't wake Chloë up. I got a hold of one of the nurses on my mother's floor and explained that I'd just had a baby and wanted to fax my mother a picture. I was put on hold. I was getting irritated, even more so when I had to fax the picture several times before a good image printed.

I finally hung up the phone, feeling physically and emotionally exhausted, not only from having given birth less than twenty-four hours earlier, but also from knowing that I'd have to support my mother emotionally. I'd have to call her several times a day, listen to her worries and complaints and try to bring up her mood. On the other hand, I was quite good at it since I'd been doing it my entire adult life, although never while trying to figure out how to take care of an hours-old baby.

I just wanted to lie down before Chloë's next feeding. The doorbell buzzed, and Vinz let in the *kraamhulp*. She came in, said hello and chatted for a few minutes and then practically pushed me to my bedroom. There, she checked my temperature and asked how I was feeling. She put a sleeping Chloë in her bassinette and left me in my bedroom, alone with my thoughts. As the *kraamhulp* vacuumed the living room, I felt myself dozing off; however, I couldn't quite fall asleep, because I kept thinking about my mother.

I was indignant. Who was she to barge in on my moment? It was my turn to bask in the glory of motherhood. As my mother, she should have been telling me how proud she was that I'd accomplished such a feat. She should have been grateful that I'd finally given her the grandchild she'd been pestering me about. Indignation was slowly giving rise to anger. I'd always envisioned her being there for me, listening to my fears and doubts, reassuring me that I'd be a great mother and that everything was going to turn out fine. Yet, there I was, just like always, having to be strong for *her.* My anger soon found its outlet in tears. Whether I was crying out of disappointment and resentment or because of the hormones, I'll never know, but the tears gushing out gave way to a rush of memories about my mother as intense as the contractions I'd endured only hours ago, before I became a mother myself.

Recollecting past events involving my mother, my head justified her leaning on me with the full weight of her depressions and disappointments. She hadn't been on good terms with my father and had withdrawn from her family, so who else did she have to turn to besides me? My heart, on the other hand, reminded me that I'd had a right to my childhood and youth. Helping my mother carry her load had forced me to grow up way too fast, which wasn't fair to me. But thinking about the gravity of her situation had the same effect on me as it always had: I felt unforgivably guilty for being so selfish as to think about myself and my own needs.

Just months before leaving New Orleans, I'd been talking to my mother on the phone about nothing in particular when, from out of nowhere, she'd dropped a bomb on my head. She had informed me that she was schizophrenic.

"What do you mean you're schizophrenic?" I'd asked her, nearly dropping the phone.

"That's what my psychiatrist just told me," she'd said, sounding a bit confused.

"Mom," I almost yelled into the receiver, "this isn't something that just happened to you. I don't understand. You always said you were depressed. Are you sure that's what he said?"

"I don't know. Thelma used to tell me that I was sick. But she never told me what was wrong with me."

"But didn't you ever ask any of your doctors? How could you not know about something like this?" I scolded.

Her revelation had stunned me. Her lack of agency had pissed me off. Who went through life with such a serious mental illness and not know about it? She'd had four kids for God's sake. How could she go from being depressed about Cory and Dawn's deaths to that? How could she reach the age of sixty-one without knowing something like that?

Still rattled by the end of our conversation, I'd sat at my desk in the den and turned on my computer. I got on to the internet and started typing "s-c-h-i-t-s ..." I couldn't even spell it; I had to look it up in my dictionary. What I'd read about the way the illness manifested itself in a person's daily life didn't affect me as much as reading that it was hereditary. I'd begun to think about all the times I'd felt depressed. Could I also become schizophrenic? Should I ask a psychiatrist to test me for schizophrenia? Instead, I'd called my father because he had worked in a facility for the mentally ill. As an educator, he'd spent years researching ways to teach patients with severe mental illnesses. He'd certainly be able to tell me something, anything.

I called him and asked straight out why he'd never told me my mother was basically psychotic.

"I don't think your mother's schizophrenic, Carolyn. People with that illness hallucinate and have to be hospitalized," he said, perhaps trying to convince himself that his ex-wife and mother of his children couldn't have been that seriously ill without him knowing about it. But he hadn't known, even though he'd been married to her for ten years and had had two children with her. He hadn't known.

Instead of being lulled to sleep by the *kraamhulp's* shuffling about in the living room, I lay awake thinking about my baby girl. What were the chances that she'd be diagnosed with that scary illness? Hadn't my mother always told me that these things skipped a generation? Even if I were safe from its ravages, would my beautiful daughter be? Had my mother ever had the same worry about me? I lay awake recollecting events that I'd witnessed and others that

I'd experienced vicariously through my mother's own words. Like the time she was visiting my grandmother, who'd lived on the third floor of an apartment building for the elderly.

"Something told me to pick up the butcher knife in the kitchen and kill her with it," my mother had told me one time, her eyes staring almost blankly at me. "I was so scared; I didn't want to kill my mother," she went on. "The door was open, so I ran out to get away from that voice. I walked over to a set of windows in the hallway and opened one. I wanted to get away from that voice so I climbed out and stood on the ledge. I guess I stood there for a long time because I remember seeing a man on the ground looking up at me yelling to me to go back inside. But I was scared of the voice inside, so I jumped."

Listening to her account, I'd imagined the wild look in her eyes as she scrambled to stand up on a broken ankle. She'd told me that she was afraid the man was going to call the police on her and that she'd be put away.

"I knew they'd take you all away from me," she continued.

She didn't even know how she managed to find a phone and call her youngest brother to pick her up and take her to the hospital. She'd obviously made it home because I remember trying to figure out how they'd put on the cast, which extended from her ankle to her thigh.

Then there was one my earliest childhood memories. It was in the middle of the night, and I had been looking down at my bare feet, shivering, wondering why my mother, sisters and I had been crouched down in our next-door neighbor's back yard. It was cold and it was dark and I didn't understand how I'd gone from sleeping in the warm bed I'd shared with Dawn, to hiding out next door. After what seemed like hours, my mother had taken us back inside our own apartment and sat us down at the dining room table.

"Tommy's trying to kill us," she'd explained calmly and reasonably, at least to my seven-year-old ears. "If you see him, run." Tommy was her third brother and had had some run-ins with the law, so it had been plausible that he might be after us. "I think we're all safe now," she'd said before sending us back to bed.

My earliest childhood memory was my mother's hallucination.

Unsolicited memories kept knocking on the door of my consciousness, reminding me that I'd been an unwilling witness to several of my mother's nervous breakdowns, one that was public. I couldn't have been more than eight or nine, which is probably why I had no clue as to why she would be sprawled outside our apartment, pounding her fists on the sidewalk, screaming out some of the most personal and embarrassing events of her life. The whole apartment complex must have gathered around to witness that spectacle, much like they were watching some reality TV series. I, on the other hand, was watching something that had been too crazy to be real.

A year, maybe two, after finding out what was "wrong" with my mother, I'd asked her how she had managed to keep us kids. Without the slightest hesitation she said, "I don't know, Carolyn. I don't know. I just knew I had to keep you girls." I wept for my mother, unable to imagine the weight of raising children alone, of losing two children alone and fighting to stay out of a mental institution – alone. The injustice of her life had crushed me.

Chloë's whimper brought me back to my reality. I lifted my head to see her sleeping soundly and then to turn over my tear-wet pillow. Despite the heaviness that had invaded my heart, I knew I had to make a choice because my mother's load had become unbearable. I had to choose between my newborn baby girl, who needed me for her very existence, and my own mother who'd already existed a lifetime. Chloë needed me to teach her how to live; my mother needed me to be her emotional crutch. I had to let go. But, how could I let go of the one person who had fought her way through insanity just to hold on to me?

In those few hours, motherhood had bestowed upon me the divine gift of forgiveness. For years I'd been pissed off at my mother, blaming her for my insecurities, my pessimistic attitude toward my life, for stealing my childhood. I'd resented her choosing me to support her and inspire her to keep living when she'd wondered what she had to live for. In the few short hours after Chloë's birth, I understood what I couldn't understand before: a mother would protect her child, even from herself. My anger had finally subsided, allowing me to redefine my relationship with my mother.

I would choose for my daughter, just as my mother had chosen for hers.

*U*nder the best circumstances, becoming a mother is intense. The changes occurring in my and

Vinz's lives immediately after claiming this new role, magnified that intensity to such a degree that it was hard to believe I'd made it through that first year with my sanity, let alone with any iota of confidence in myself as a mother, academic or even as a black woman. After moving back to Holland, Vinz had left the hotel industry and worked his way up from an operations supervisor to area manager at a leading security company, which meant he was preoccupied with settling into his new position. Settling into our new house, which we'd bought shortly after returning from Cuba, was to become my preoccupation, a task that I took on grudgingly.

In retrospect, we should've kept our butts put in our fifth-floor apartment with the spectacular view until Chloë was a year old, but we just *had* to move into a house. Perhaps we'd both been nesting. Perhaps the Dutch belief that a backyard went hand in hand with having a child had forced itself into Vinz's mind. To me a home had symbolized every single aspect of the childhood that I never had: a stable family life, the comforts that money bought and the privileges that, in my America, were extended only to white people. Neither of my parents had ever owned a home so I should have been pleased that I was living the

American dream of surpassing my parents. I never expected to resent owning a home, especially after having lived in apartments my whole life.

The house that took us two months to find and close on was nothing special. We'd bought it because it was located in Voorschoten, a surprisingly international village between Leiden and The Hague. Typical of Dutch houses built in the 1960s, our living area was rectangular, with very little potential to turn it into our showplace. The kitchen was depressingly small with white linoleum countertops and matching cabinets. The centerpiece was a bulky white water boiler, which hung smack dab in the middle of the wall opposite the dining area, and was distasteful enough to cause indigestion even in the strongest of stomachs.

Wallpaper had been layered on every available wall. The brown and orange floral pattern adorning the top layer was unsightly, to say the least. The two layers beneath were so ugly, we understood why the previous owners had papered on top of them. The wood floor must have been beautiful forty years ago. The harsh sunlight had faded the panels around the windows, which consumed two of the three outside walls. We could see shiny nails poking their heads through the worn surface, which had obviously never been replaced.

The second floor was, arguably, in better shape. The bedrooms were relatively spacious and equipped with built-in closets, a rarity in Dutch houses. However, the bathroom was so small we couldn't fit a bathtub in it. To create a smidgeon of space, we took out the toilet and installed it in the hall closet that we renovated just for that purpose. The attic, though spacious, was unfinished, and since our funds were nearly finished, it would remain uninhabited.

By the time we'd moved into the house, the old kitchen had already been torn out. Unfortunately, the new kitchen would not be arriving for another three weeks, which meant depending on the kindness of our friends for meals. They must have been more relieved than we were when our kitchen was finally installed. No cooking for three solid weeks should have been a welcome respite from my new domestic duties, but after only a few days, it was a pain in the ass. Even when we ate take out, we still needed to wash the cups and silverware, which we did upstairs in our tiny bathroom. The only good thing was that I was nursing Chloë, so there were no bottles to refrigerate or heat up.

Shortly after the kitchen was in place, work had begun on our windows, every one of which had to be removed and replaced by double glass and new frames. It was the beginning of November, and I was cold. The three strange men doing the renovations tracked dirt on my newly laid carpet, talked loudly while Chloë tried to nap and generally robbed me of my peace of mind. It didn't help that I was obligated by Dutch etiquette to make coffee for the men running in and out of my house.

Besides dealing with the physical irritations and inconveniences in our new home, I suffered some emotional kickback. I'd always felt embarrassed that I'd never lived in a house, so I should have felt grateful that my child had something that I never had. But I didn't. In fact, I felt lonely. I hadn't yet built up my own network of friends. I hadn't gotten to know my new village yet, so I'd go back to Leiden for most of my necessaries. I didn't have a car and Chloë was too young to tote around on a bike the Dutch way, so my only means of transportation was the bus. The problem was that my stroller was too wide to fit in the narrow aisle of some of the older buses. More than once I'd had to wait an extra half hour for the next bus, hoping it was a newer one with wider aisles. Plus, at that time of year, the weather was cold enough for the constant rain and gray skies to chill me to the bone. Needless to say, I shut myself up inside for most of the day.

Vinz didn't get home from work until early evening. His parents lived an hour and a half away. His sister who had put us up when we'd just arrived had her own family to take care of, so I couldn't expect her to come to my rescue. True, my girlfriends were but a phone call away, but the time difference made it virtually impossible to connect with them. I longed to live close enough to my mother to be able to drop Chloë off for a few hours while I just got out of the house and spent some time by myself.

But, even if I could talk to my own family and friends, what on earth would I say to them? That I felt isolated inside my new home? That I couldn't cope even though I had a husband, one child and a good job that paid me to be home with her for five months? How many black women – teen-aged black women at that – had managed to make it without the fathers of their children? I'd watched my own mother struggle with very little support from my father or from her family. She'd made it on her own and, by God, so should I.

So I said nothing.

Contrary to what society would have us believe, the bonding between a mother and her baby doesn't always happen instantly. The dominant image I'd had during my pregnancy was of me gazing lovingly at the wrapped bundle cuddled up in my arms. Her eyes would meet mine as she suckled my breast then raise her tiny hand to caress my face. Having been the youngest and having had no experience with babies, I clung to Hollywood's depiction of motherhood as being something that all women wanted and were instinctively good at.

My ideal pregnancy had done little to dispel that myth of motherhood. Besides feeling tired during the first trimester, I never experienced any other symptom of pregnancy. I'd never gotten morning sickness or swollen ankles. My only craving was for fruit, so the only place I'd gained weight was in my belly. During the second and third trimesters, I had so much energy I'd cycled the ten kilometers to and from the train stations to get to work up until I had to go on maternity leave. I'd even wanted to work up until a week before my due date, but Dutch law had required me to stop working a minimum of four weeks prior. I'd felt so good I persuaded my boss to let me teach a literature course the semester following my leave. That I'd never taught world literature before and that it was outside my specialization hadn't mattered to me. The pregnancy had been so effortless I figured I could accomplish anything. I'd have five months off, so I just knew I'd have plenty of time to prepare for that course as well as finish writing my dissertation.

Please.

Nothing had prepared me for the disruption ... nay ... the utter chaos that motherhood had delivered to my new doorstep. My midwife had obviously forgotten to explain that I'd be waking up every two hours, in the middle of the night, to nurse my baby. She'd left out the part about being pissed off at Vinz when I heard him snoring at 2:00 am, his sleep not interrupted by Chloë's cries for nourishment. None of the pro-breastfeeding literature that I'd read had bothered to inform me that hormones, necessary to produce the milk, would also affect my emotional stability. None of my friends had mentioned that I might get a baby that didn't sleep. During the day Chloë was one of those babies who slept only when and if I was holding her. The minute I laid her down, she'd wake up screaming until I picked her up again. I spent hours sitting, trapped on the couch, holding her in my arms, afraid to reach for the remote control lest that slight movement awaken her. I hated motherhood.

Nor did I immediately fall in love with my
Chloë. I wasn't even sure I liked her at first. She didn't
sleep, but she sure cried a lot. Most of the time I had no
idea what to do for her, so I convinced myself that the
universe had made a mistake by making me a mother.
My mother-in-law (bless her heart) had suggested that
maybe Chloë's crying was a reaction to my insecurity.
I turned her advice to trust myself into just another
reason to believe I wasn't mother material. I reasoned
that Chloë didn't care who was holding her as long
as a pair of arms comforted her. The milk from my
neighbor's ample bosom would have doused her
hunger pangs as well as my little B-cup breast. Would
she have noticed if I'd fallen off the face of the earth if
someone were there to love her? Probably not. What
was wrong with me?

With each cry from Chloë, the identity that
I'd spent thirty-six years building was shattered. I had
been reduced to trying to figure out why my baby was
crying because, unlike all those other women who
could instinctively differentiate their babies' cries, all
her cries sounded the same to me. Needless to say,
the only time I had to read the novels in preparation
for teaching my course was right before I went to

bed. Alas, I'd fall asleep after the first ten pages or so because I was just plain tuckered out by the end of the day. That I hadn't written nary a word on my dissertation since delivering Chloë just added guilt to the emotions swirling around inside me like Dorothy's cyclone, steadily gaining momentum.

For the first time in our relationship, tension arose between Vinz and me. Our racial and cultural differences had never been an issue between us. Marriage didn't change anything. Vinz was so caught up in his new job that he didn't stop to think that I might need help at home in my new job. He simply didn't understand that I was losing myself, and because he didn't understand, he never asked. He assumed I was doing something wrong, and I knew this based on his suggestions that I not nurse her on demand, perhaps she was crying because she had gas bubbles as a result of being fed too often. Maybe I shouldn't hold her so much and just let her cry for a while.

The truth was, I had invested so much of my energy in creating an identity as an academic. Studying and university life were all I knew. Through junior high and high school, I'd basked in mother's praise whenever I got good grades, which was all the time. I'd met some of my closest friends at school. I knew myself when I was on a university campus. I was confident when I was in front of a classroom. My sense of humor and my intelligence had an outlet in discussions with colleagues. Why was motherhood demanding I throw that all away? In my mind getting back to work meant getting back to myself. But I still had two more months of the hell on earth that was maternity leave.

January 12, 2004 finally arrived. At 7:20 am I wheeled my bike out of the shed, opened the backyard gate and cycled the three kilometers to the train station feeling like I'd survived the Apocalypse. I could have jumped up and down and danced a jig while I sang my gratitude at going back to work. Sure, I worried about Chloë's wellbeing at daycare. Yes, I was afraid that her *leidsters* would let her cry longer than I would or that one of the toddlers in her group would pinch her. But cycling for the first time in five months was enough to remind me of the rhythm of my days before I became a mother.

Once at the station in Leiden, I left my bike in the small *fietsenstalling*, or parking garage for bikes, climbed the single flight of stairs to the platform, bought a week's worth of tickets and waited for my train. The other passengers must have been wondering why on earth I was beaming as I boarded the train for the forty-five minute commute to Utrecht. I knew why. Walking through the dank *fietsenstalling* underneath Utrecht's *Centraal Station* to pick up my second bike, which I had stored there, I smiled at the familiar musty odor that used to turn my nose, but on that day I felt relieved that nothing had changed during the five months that I'd been away.

On my way to my own bike, I spotted one decorated with multicolored smiley faces and laughed out loud. I immediately recalled my original impression of that *fietsenstalling*. There had been so many bikes that I'd felt like I'd walked into a hall of mirrors like the one in the final fighting scene in *Enter the Dragon* where Bruce Lee was reflected twenty times and neither the viewer nor the sinister Han knew which was the real one. Then, I'd seen bikes painted the most unbecoming shade of orange or highlighted with butterfly stickers. How I'd scorned the Dutch for their involvement with their bikes. The joke, however, had been on me: bike decorating wasn't just a gratuitous activity. On the contrary, its purpose was to quickly and easily identify one's bicycle out of the hundreds also parked in the garage. That first time I'd spent the better part of fifteen minutes searching for my own unmarked bike.

Within seconds the green and yellow striped duct tape that I'd used to cover my seat jumped out at me as if to say, "long time no see". I wheeled it toward the exit, cycling through a *fietsenstalling* being prohibited, and once outside, cycled the fifteen minutes to campus. The university's administration building, which housed my office, had been closed for the winter holiday. My first day back had also been the first day back for my colleagues, so the atmosphere was relaxed. I spent the day drinking endless cups of tea, greeting my colleagues and chatting with them about being a mother and about how good it felt to be back. I was enthusiastic about seeing my students and getting back into the classroom even though I'd only made a lesson plan for the first class. I wasn't at all worried because I'd never planned my classes too far in advance. Surely, I could read the required novels on my days off and prepare at night after Chloë had gone to sleep. If necessary, I could even pull an all-nighter just like in the old days.

I left campus feeling tired but optimistic. I cycled to the train station feeling light and not a little carefree, unaware that it would be the last time for a long time that I would experience such levity. Unfortunately, that first day back belied the reality of being a working mother, a role that would push my already fragile self-image over the edge, shattering it into the countless fragments that had existed inside me. I'd be forced to pick up each one, examine it closely and find a way to reattach it to a brand new whole.

In the weeks that followed, I found myself in a torrid affair with my alarm clock. Poor Vinz. At 6:00 am he was still fast asleep and had no clue that my snooze button was shamelessly flirting with me. I of course played hard to get, paying attention to my clock's face only after the alarm had gone off three times. From that moment on, my bedside lover was replaced by my new love, who slept in her bassinette a few inches away from my bed. At six months Chloë continued to wake up once or twice in the middle of the night to be nursed, so having her close to me was convenient. I'd also become attached to her and couldn't bear the thought of her sleeping in her own room. I peeked at her peaceful face before grabbing my robe from the bedroom closet and padding to the bathroom to brush my teeth and take a quick shower. I put my clothes on and woke Chloë up. I nursed her, cuddled with her and dressed her. If I was lucky, I had fifteen minutes to pack her bag for daycare, eat my breakfast, make my thermos of coffee for the train ride, get my papers together and walk out the door at 7:20 am. Normally, though, I had ten minutes to do all that, and usually ran out the door. Luckily, Vinz dropped Chloë off at daycare so that I could catch my train on time.

My days had fallen into a new routine revolving around not sleeping, rushing around in the morning to catch my train, teach and advise students and then rush home again to pick Chloë up on time. Since I got home first, I usually bought groceries and cooked dinner. While Vinz cleaned up, I gave Chloë her bath, nursed and cuddled her and put her to bed. I rarely thought about writing a lesson plan before 8:00 pm, and that was only after I'd graded homework or made the schedule for my students' presentations. I hadn't read most of the novels on my syllabus, so I had to read along with my students. In order to prepare my lectures, I had read article after article to understand the context of the novels and to try to anticipate my students' questions. By 11:00 pm I was bushed. Still, I had one more feeding before I could slide into my bed.

Although I only worked three days a week, I felt like I'd been putting in overtime rushing from one thing to the next.

One morning I did something different: I sat down at the table with my bowl of cereal and started weeping without understanding why. True, I was exhausted. True, I was intimidated by my students, most of them in their freshman year. On more than one occasion I'd been asked a question that I simply couldn't answer. One student had made a comment about the end of a novel we were reading. The blank look on my face told her that I hadn't finished it, and she called me out on it. Midterms were approaching, which meant I had to meet with each of the forty students I was advising. I'd have to put in extra hours to accomplish that, which meant less time to prepare for my course. And yet, I couldn't figure out why tears were dripping off my chin and plopping into my muesli.

Later that day, I talked to the senior tutor about the difficulties I was having teaching a course that I had no academic background in, and she advised me to invite a few colleagues to lecture on the material that I had the least experience with. As for my advising duties, she suggested I spend a few minutes less with each student at midterm so that I wouldn't have to put in so much overtime. Having taught in Poland, America and Holland, she was experienced. She was an ally who knew her way around, so I left her office feeling relieved.

By the time I sat down at my desk, I'd already dismissed her advice. It was bad enough that I'd let her in on my dirty little secret. Up to that point I'd successfully masked my anxiety behind a bright smile. The stacks of books in the bookcase next to my desk and the growing mound of papers on it hinted at an industriousness that was little more than busy work. Asking colleagues to step foot in my classroom, even as guest speakers, was inviting them to witness my incompetence. Besides, where was I going to find someone to help me right then? I had to teach in a couple of hours. I still had to go over my lesson plan and review the notes I'd written on what I'd read the night before.

The dull ache in my breasts reminded me I needed to pump off the milk that I would put in Chloë's daycare bag the next day. The dull ache in my stomach reminded me I still needed to eat my lunch. I grabbed my cheese sandwich and apple and walked downstairs to the kitchen. I placed the bottle, the breast funnel and the hand pump into the plastic sterilizer and put it in the microwave for ninety seconds. I opened the lid, which resembled the cover of a cake plate, and out wafted the scent of burnt plastic. I could not believe what I'd done. The hand pump was not microwave-proof, and it had melted. My heart sank. If I didn't pump off that milk, Chloë wouldn't have any food the following day. I cursed our decision to postpone introducing formula to her diet. *"What are you gonna do?"* asked my voice. The only thing I could do: return to my office and cry. When she saw my face, my office mate jumped from her chair and gently placed her arm around my shoulders. By the time I finished explaining my predicament, a small, wet circle was forming on my blouse. I hadn't had time to buy breast pads.

She dropped what she was doing and drove me into town so I could spend fifty euros on another pump – and two boxes of pads. We drove back to campus with time enough for me to relieve the pressure on my chest, borrow a sweater and teach my class. Unbeknownst to me, it would be the last time I received any support from my colleagues.

On the bike ride back to the train station at the end of the day, the voice in my head that had become both my best friend and my worst enemy, added her two cents about how my day had gone in particular and my emotional state in general during those first few months as a working mother.

"*What's the matter with you?*" she scolded. "*Get it together. You're a strong black woman,*" she continued, "*and we've been through much worse than this.*"

I fought back the tears for most of the forty-five minute train ride home. I refused to admit to myself that I wasn't coping. I'd wanted to talk about my work situation with Vinz, but I couldn't bring myself to approach him. He was progressing in his career, so I assumed he'd criticize me for being so weak. I thought he'd compare me to his own mother, who always knew what to do when we called for parenting advice, and find me wanting. Nor could I talk to my own mother. She'd worked full time and raised my sisters and me with no help. Several of my friends had also been single mothers, and they managed. What was wrong with me that I couldn't?

"So much for carrying the torch," I finally replied to the voice in my head. I asked myself what kind of a black woman would break down in tears over a breast pump. A real black woman would have put those rich little white kids in their place for calling her out in public. I didn't deserve to wear my skin. As the train made its first stop in Woerden, it hit me that I hadn't felt this unworthy of my blackness since high school and college.

*I*n some ways the transition to high school had been smooth. North Central High was directly behind my junior high school so the shock of the half-hour bus ride to the white side of town had already worn off. I'd made the flag corps and ran varsity track. My mother had helped me decide that I wanted to be a doctor so I knew I'd have to keep my grades up, which I did. I was consistently on the high honor roll or honor roll, which hadn't been difficult since I loved school. My favorite classes were Spanish, French and English, and I didn't do too badly in biology and chemistry.

As in all high schools, social cliques abounded at mine. We all knew who the rich kids were; the cheerleaders and pom pon girls were the most popular and the social clubs were unmistakably white. Until A.Q.U.I.L.L.A. came on the scene. I'd unfortunately not been invited to join North Central's first and only all black social club and hadn't been privy to what the acronym actually stood for. I hadn't known what the club itself stood for. I did know that the members were all black girls, so why hadn't I been invited to join?

After all, I was black. Or was I?

How many times had I heard comments about the way I spoke? Yes, I spoke grammatically correct English. I enunciated my words. I was articulate so I was proper. People had assumed that I was scared of boys because I didn't date. They'd assumed that I didn't date because I always had my head in the books. But I'd studied because I liked school and because I didn't have a wild social life. In my high-school-girl's mind, I wasn't black enough because I was too smart, I didn't like boys and I talked proper.

Feeling inferior had accompanied me to Indiana University, where I would be confronted with the relationship between money and color. Up to that point, my worldview had linked wealth with whiteness. Sure, I'd run into a few blacks whose families had a little bit of money, but at IU I'd I felt out of my league. Other black people I'd run into on campus wore the same expensive sweatshirts with the college's emblem as the white kids did. I couldn't even afford to buy my books. Despite the fact that my mother's people had had status as doctors, lawyers, dentists and that my father and his brothers were well educated, I felt like I couldn't compete.

I lived in the dorm my freshman year and

roomed with Lisa, a black girl who I'd twirled flags with in high school. When I'd discovered she'd also been on her way to IU, I'd suggested we share a room. Good thing too, because she'd been gracious enough to let me borrow her books for the *History of Medicine* course we'd both registered for. She'd paid for our loft and the tiny refrigerator we'd rented until I'd gotten the money from my parents to repay her. Lisa had been my emotional mainstay during those first few months in an unfamiliar world.

Lisa had also told me about the Kappa Sweethearts. The Kappas, Alphas, Sigmas and Omegas were the main black fraternities on the IU campus, and their "little sisters", or sweethearts, would organize events for them and attend all their functions. Most importantly, becoming a sweetheart meant gaining admittance into IU's black social scene. I'd even had a trump card up my sleeve: my mother's uncle, Dr. Guy Grant, had been a founding father of IU's chapter of Kappa Alpha Psi fraternity. Touting my lineage would surely have given me enough status to breeze through the interview process. Unfortunately, I had to withdraw my application when I found out about the $200 membership fee.

I'd spent all of my first semester in college studying and finding other ways to build up my social life. Fraternities and sororities were vital to IU's social scene. The main drawbacks to the system were financial and racial. I could barely afford to eat on Sunday night, when the dorm cafeteria was closed, so I had no idea where was I going to find money to pledge a sorority, let alone the funds to pay for all the events that accompanied joining a sorority. The other thing was that the greeks, as they were referred to back then, were cliquish and segregated. I didn't feel like I'd fit in, so I dropped that plan.

Towards the end of my freshman year, I'd heard that the other Lisa who lived on our floor was looking for roommates to live with her off campus in the newly built condominium complex right across the street from Memorial Stadium, IU's football stadium. I'd talked to Lisa about my moving in the following school year, and she seemed receptive to the idea. I already knew the other two girls who'd be sharing the condo since they'd also lived on the same floor of the dorm. Yet I was reluctant. Lisa, who's father had invested in the condo, was from Carmel, a small city just north of Indianapolis, infamous for its lack of blacks. Needless to say, I was wary of her because I never knew when she was going to get mad at me and call me a nigger. But up to that point she never had, so I took a chance.

My concern had been for naught because Lisa had a natural sweetness about her that bordered on naivety. She was sincere in her efforts to accept me at face value. She was willing to live with a black girl so how prejudiced could she be? I would spend hours arguing with her over the most inconsequential topics. Our backgrounds had been so different that our perspectives had no other option but to clash.

And clash they did, especially when we'd discussed the Vanessa Williams scandal. She'd been the first black Miss America. She'd been the only Miss America I'd heard of who'd given up her title when, shortly before her reign ended, racy photos of her, some involving another woman, had surfaced. At her press conference, she'd given the most memorable statement when she'd proclaimed, "I'm not a lesbian, and I'm not a whore." In my opinion, she'd been forced to relinquish her title because she was black. Had she been white, I'd argued, those photos wouldn't have been allowed to circulate. Lisa argued adamantly that racism had had nothing to do with the scandal.

We'd argued back and forth until one of our other roommates, Juli, jumped in and argued that the fact that Ms. Williams had won in the first place nullified any talk of racism.

Juli, who was also white, had grown up in Terre Haute, about an hour west of Indianapolis. I'd always considered it a hick town, and by extension the people were all rednecks. Juli, however, was the coolest white girl I'd ever met, and we clicked. Maybe it was because she didn't come from money and knew what it was like to struggle. Maybe it was because she liked me for who I was. I don't know why we clicked, but I could confide in her and found myself telling her things about my life that I hadn't shared with anyone else, not even my mother. She would become a true soul mate.

My third roommate was Jamie, who'd grown up in Indianapolis and apparently had gone to the same high school as I did. She'd informed me that she'd even sat next to me in our junior-year English class. "I was so jealous of your long nails," she'd told me, laughing. I had no idea who she was until we became roommates. Her father was part owner of one of the most successful and well-known car dealerships in Indianapolis, so I figured she'd never wanted for anything. Still, Jamie was unbelievably down to earth and a good person to talk to. She asked an awful lot of questions, though, which we ruthlessly teased her about.

Juli, Lisa, Jamie and I formed our own little sorority. We looked out for each other and supported one another through break-ups and bad grades. We'd pull all-nighters at the Denny's on I-37 or stay up working on a puzzle or playing euchre and spades. Through Lisa I got a job as an assistant secretary at the College Mall office and through Juli I got a job as a party photographer. The only camera I'd ever picked up was a Polaroid, but that didn't stop me from working at Greek functions as though I were a professional.

Juli had gotten an assignment to shoot pictures at a Kappa Alpha Psi formal event, and asked me if I wanted to tag along.

"I'll tell them you're my assistant and that I'm training you. I have an old camera you can use. It doesn't have a flash, but we'll say you're just learning the ropes."

Here was my chance to experience black social life on campus. But once I arrived at the function, I knew that deep down I wanted to be accepted in that circle. I hoped the Kappa brothers would extend an invitation to join the Sweethearts; I wanted the women of Alpha Kappa Alpha, a black sorority, to consider pledging me when they took their next line. But when I saw the pretty ladies wearing their formal dresses slow dancing with fine Kappas decked out in their tuxedos I saw myself as the quintessential girl on the outside looking in, a kid with her nose pressed against the candy store window. I wasn't one of them; I was an imposter who'd crashed their party pretending to be something I was not.

All this was happening around the premier of *A Different World*, which was the spin-off of *The Cosby Show*. It centered around Denise, the free-spirited, second oldest Huxtable child during her first years at the fictional black school, Hillman College. She'd been my favorite character on *The Cosby Show* because she was cool, beautiful and alternative. Lisa Bonet, the actress who portrayed her, was biracial but had her own style that seemed to transcend her race. I would have sold my soul to the devil to be her, to have good hair and light skin.

Ironically, I had never fantasized about being white, nor did I *hate* my blackness. To my mind, being mixed was a way to access the white world while still holding on to the black community. I thought that all my heartaches could have been alleviated if only I were mixed because I would have grown up with a mother and a father, all the boys would have been after me and I would have been asked to join all the social clubs. I'd have had money and access to the college of my choice, just like Denise Huxtable.

By this point the mixed messages I'd received from the black community and white America had me feeling so insecure about my body image that I had trouble looking in mirrors, especially in bars (after I'd turned twenty-one, of course) or at parties where white girls were brushing their blond locks, reapplying pink lipstick and discussing the virtues of that week's fraternity boy. I'd never learned how to put on blush and thought lipstick made my lips look too big. The chance that my hair had frizzed and puffed up prevented me from checking myself out, so I'd just wash my hands as quickly as possible and leave the restroom without ever making eye contact with the other girls. Or with myself. How ugly I felt.

By my third year in college, Denise Huxtable had rubbed off on me. I tried to become racially and culturally ambiguous. All that I'd learned from the black community went to the wayside. I hung out exclusively with my white roommates, stopped going to the beauty shop, which I couldn't afford anyway, wore long skirts and combat boots. I even started messing around with white boys. I'd never been interested in dating outside my race despite my mother's constant admonitions about marrying a black man. "I married two good-for-nothing black men who never did a damn thing for me. You make sure you get yourself a white man, you hear me?" she'd repeated constantly.

And maybe she'd been right. I'd already gotten sick and tired of random black men undressing me with their lecherous eyes as though they had every right to that violation simply because I was a sister. I was fed up with being whistled at and talked to like I was being claimed as communal property by virtue of my skin color. I'd actually become afraid of expressing my sexuality, so I covered up my legs, which my mother had always admired, and shrouded my other goods in bulky sweaters, baggy pants and weird outfits that no self-respecting black girl would have been caught dead in. I was dressing like many of the white girls I'd seen on campus.

I had desexualized myself hoping that black men would turn their unwanted attention from me. But that wasn't the most reprehensible part. I felt like

I couldn't vocalize my shame. Had I dared suggest that I didn't appreciate that type of attention, I'd have been accused of being a sell-out. The lascivious looks would have turned into verbal attacks that I "thought I was too good to speak to a brotha". I'd already heard that a girl from my high school had commented that "Carolyn isn't black anymore; she hangs out with white people." I kept my mouth shut and went into a self-imposed exile from the black community and took refuge in the white, where androgyny was acceptable and sexuality forbidden (so I believed), the only safe place for a black girl like me who needed to get away from the expectations of black people regarding the way I spoke, who I had sex with, the grades I got, who my friends should be, which sports I could play, what music I could listen to, and the list goes on.

Once there I stumbled upon a rebelliousness that had obviously been lurking behind the insecure, proper-talking girl who liked to study. I started smoking and drinking beer at parties. For the first time in my life, my grades fell, never to recover, which gave me the perfect excuse to drop out of my (mother's) long-time dream of medical school. I knew I'd be disappointing my mother, the one person who had always insisted I had the brains to be anything I wanted. But at the same time, I refused to acquiesce to my mother, the one person who'd raised me with so many contradictory messages that I hadn't the slightest idea who I was or what I wanted to become. She didn't understand that the once easy math and science were killing me. She didn't know that I couldn't even stand the sight of blood. And there was that needle thing. I ended up majoring in Spanish because it came easy to me, and I liked it. Good thing I did because it gave me the perfect opportunity to study in Mexico.

The summer before my senior year had been a turning point for what I believed was my place in the world. I'd applied for a summer program in Guanajuato, Mexico, where I would live with a host family and immerse myself in Mexican culture. Luckily, my financial aid package covered the tuition and room and board with a little left over for entertainment. Not once had I considered that I'd be more or less alone in a foreign country. I hadn't cared that I'd probably be the only black person in the entire country. I just knew it was an opportunity to experience firsthand a culture I'd only read about in books and speak a language I'd only used in a classroom setting. I knew it was a chance to step outside of black and white America.

The other exchange students and chaperones were gathering and flying out of Chicago, but for some reason I ended up flying separately from Indianapolis. I'd never been on an airplane before, and there I was traveling to Mexico all by myself. I got off the plane in Mexico City, and all my courage seemed to vanish behind the thick curtain of smoke that filled the grubby airport. I stood in one spot for what seemed like an hour looking around for something familiar. I had no idea when the others would arrive, nor did I know how to get to Guanajuato in case I missed the group. I spotted an information booth, but I didn't walk toward it. Instead, my eyes began to water as I tried – and failed – to come up with the Spanish words to ask for my group's arrival time.

On the other hand, I couldn't stand in the corner all day waiting for who-knew-what to happen, so I forced my jelly-like legs to stand solid while I collected my meager luggage. I noticed a small brown-skinned man dressed in gray pants and a blue shirt approaching me. He stopped right in front of me and began speaking Spanish. When it was clear to him that I had no clue what he was saying, he pointed to my bags and said in broken and heavily accented English, "Ay carry you bag?"

I wondered why would he want to carry my bags around. Before I could find an answer to my silent question, he picked them up and started walking. I followed him as he seemed to know where he was going. Once outside, he put down the bags, at which point my tongue finally sprang into action. "Gracias, señor," I muttered and looked away, dismissing him unknowingly. He didn't walk away. When I looked at him again, he said, holding out his hand, "My teep?" I fumbled around my pocket for a dollar, mentally kicking myself for not understanding and swearing that I'd go to all my Spanish classes once I got back to IU.

Feeling like the world's biggest *pendeja*, the word Mexicans use for idiot, I picked up my bags and marched right back inside the airport and to the information desk, where I managed to discover that my group's plane had landed. Needless to say, I successfully met up with them and made it to Guanajuato with everything intact, except for my pride of course.

The two things that stood out for me while I was in Guanajuato were the poverty and warmth of the people. I'd never seen beggars before, so I was blown away by the toothless, crippled man I saw sitting on a sidewalk, his cupped hand lifted toward indifferent passersby. And I just couldn't make heads or tails of dirty children, dressed in rags, asking total strangers for money. As poor as we'd been, we never lived on the streets. We may have eaten only rice and grits for days at a time, but we ate. We'd had heating, beds to sleep in and we'd been clean.

That summer in Guanajuato there were days when I couldn't take a shower because there was no water. I wore the same clothes days in a row because the water tank at the Laundromat was empty. My host family had just moved to Guanajuato from Mexico City and had yet to have their phone installed. They'd been considered well off because they could afford a telephone. In the meantime if I wanted to make a local call to one of my friends in the exchange program, I had to walk a few hundred yards to the neighborhood payphone. To call my mother or my roommates, I had to go to a *casera* in town, where I'd buy what's known today as a presubscribed phone card and sit in an indoor phone booth. For the first time in my twenty years I'd felt fortunate. That summer I learned that there were people in the world who were worse off than me. More than once I surmised that that was how white people in America must feel.

Besides the poverty, what struck me about Mexico was its warmth, not climate-wise but people-wise. I'd never felt so welcome in my life. I was obviously a foreigner and one the people of Guanajuato hadn't been familiar seeing. On my way to class each morning, I'd leave my host family's house to walk down to the center of town. A couple hundred yards away from the house, a group of kids would be waiting to ambush me with smiles and stares. At some point they'd asked me my name and from then on "Hola, Carolina," became part of their arsenal.

As I made my way down the narrow, curving streets, passing small houses built on the slope of the mountain, I'd hear this one muttering, "*morena*," which literally means "brown girl", and that one hurling a quiet, "*buenos días, bonita*." In town I'd wait for a bus to take me up the mountain on the other side of town. The locals stared and uttered, "*Psst*," to get the attention of the *morena*, the foreigner. They didn't seem to care that I was black. They were curious about me, that was all.

They were also helpful, especially when my words got in the way of communicating. Instead of correcting my mistakes, as the Spaniards did, they tried to teach me. "*Elote*," said the dark brown woman, whose gentle smile betrayed her lack of a complete set of teeth, when I couldn't find the word to ask for my favorite snack – and the only one we Americans were allowed to buy from street vendors – fresh corn smothered in a sweet, buttery cream. We had been warned that fruit and raw vegetables had probably been washed with tap water, the bacteria in which would wreak havoc in our unaccustomed digestive tracts.

Their patience at my verbal awkwardness, as well as their utter lack of offense that I hadn't yet perfected their language, had put me as ease so that I dared to make mistakes when I spoke. By the end of the summer, my Spanish had improved so much that I was no longer self-conscious about it. Not only that, but I could feel proud of myself for being on my own and facing situations I'd never had to up until that point, like living with strangers in their home or trying to move around in a country that didn't speak my language. The beautiful part was that I'd done it. I'd managed. The world had opened its doors to me, and I'd walked through. Besides the deaths of my sister and brother very little had had such a lasting impact on my life as that summer in Mexico. Even though I wasn't from there, I never felt like I didn't belong. The stereotypes attached to blackness were not valid there. I saw for the first time that blackness didn't automatically mean the same as poverty, which empowered me to question, for the first time, what I'd learned about being a black woman in the world.

But back in Holland, my train's sudden stop lurched me from thoughts of empowerment and accomplishment. I exited the train, found my bike in the *fietsenstalling* and headed home. My run-in with the breast pump that day had opened the floodgates of distress. The pressure of standing in front of the class unprepared and non-conversant with the material had taken its toll on my emotional stability. I felt humiliated when a student, sensing my incompetence, refused to participate in classroom discussions. Other students had sniffed out my fear of being discovered to be the imposter that I was and were openly hostile. They'd circulated a petition to protest my position as their instructor.

I cycled past my house, along the train tracks and past the farm to Chloë's daycare. On my way home, I stopped at the store and bought that evening's dinner. Once at home, I nursed Chloë, cuddled and sang to her before cooking dinner. By the time I'd bathed her and put her to bed, I'd come to terms with the fact that I had to let go of something. Sending Chloë to daycare five days a week was unthinkable. I became a mother to be involved with my child's upbringing. Giving up my tutoring responsibilities wasn't an option; we needed that salary. Putting my dissertation on hold was out of consideration because I'd put too much of myself into it. Besides, I'd gone deep into debt to finance my graduate studies, and I wasn't leaving until I had that paper in my hand. The course was the logical choice. It hadn't been part of my job description, and it was eating up most of my time, consuming all of my emotional reserves. I resolved to speak with the head of the humanities department and ask him to find a replacement to finish out the semester.

It was the week before Spring Break, and I climbed into bed feeling a relief that I hadn't felt since the moment after I'd given birth to Chloë, eight months before. Vinz had taken a week off from work so the three of us could fly back to Indiana to see my mother. Seeing my childhood friends, shopping and eating familiar food were just the distractions I'd need to regroup. Since I wouldn't be teaching, I could focus all my attention on my advising duties and my dissertation. Chloë would benefit from the emotional space created from not having to worry about teaching. I knew there would be ramifications from the decision

I'd made, but I wouldn't have to deal with them for a couple of weeks. Maybe by the time everyone had returned from Spring Break, it would have blown over.

On my first day back after Spring Break, I walked into my office feeling rested and optimistic that I'd made the best decision for me. I had just turned on my computer when the senior tutor called and asked if I could come to her office for a few minutes before our weekly staff meeting. I stood up, closed the door and walked the twenty yards to her office. As soon as I entered her office, she dug in.

"I wanted to give you a heads up. Some of the other tutors are mad and may attack you in the meeting."

"Well ... what ... um ... why would they be mad at me?"

"Because you quit teaching your course."

Before I could formulate my response, she made a preemptive strike.

"I told you not to take on that course, Carolyn," she reeled. "I tried to warn you how hard it would be to commute three hours, handle your advising assignment and try to teach a new course."

I stood in front of her desk, stunned as much from the attack as the attacker. She'd been a trusted mother figure who had advised me on the ins and outs of academia, the ups and downs of motherhood, even the whys and wherefores of life. Why was she turning on me? Then came her barrage of blame.

"You're supposed to represent working mothers, Carolyn, and some of the tutors think you've ruined their chances to teach a course. What were you thinking?"

I took a few seconds to think of an explanation.

"I don't know what to say," was the best I could come up with. "Should I apologize to them?"

"I think you need to keep quiet. I don't think I can keep them from ganging up on you, so let me explain what happened," she said as she gathered her papers and walked toward the door.

"Actually, I'd like to explain my side of the story. I want them to hear it from me," I retorted. As I turned to face the firing squad, she turned the knife.

"You do realize you've ruined your career here? You'll never be allowed to teach another course?"

Despite the senior tutor's predictions, there was no attack. I said my piece and, in fact, no one seemed to care. Still, I detected an undercurrent of tension that would intensify in the days that followed.

One morning I saw a colleague standing by the communal printer and walked to her instead of going straight into my office. My friendly "how are you today?" was met with a frosty "I'm fine". She turned on her heel and walked away without looking up from the papers she held in her hand. It chilled me to the bone.

The backlash had begun.

Another colleague, who I'd shared an office with and had befriended when she came on board as a tutor the year after me, suddenly had nothing to say to me. Another one told me to my face that I had indeed ruined *her* chances of teaching because she still hadn't earned her Ph.D. True, I'd been given the opportunity to teach my own course with only a master's degree and had blown it by quitting mid-semester. However, I didn't deserve to be her scapegoat.

Backlash was bad enough, but a slap in the face was much more than I could bear. None of my male colleagues had anything to say about *my* decision to screw up *my* career. It was the women, the mothers, the working mothers who turned their backs on me. And they were all into gender equality, either academically or based on their personal politics. While I was strong and successful, I belonged to that elite club of scholars who touted feminine knowledge and female empowerment. Choosing motherhood and my own emotional balance over advancing in my career were obviously not in the club's bylaws, so when I needed guidance and support, I found my membership had been revoked.

Why hadn't I listened to the senior tutor when she'd cautioned me about teaching a new course in a subject I'd known little about so soon after becoming a new mother? That I'd underestimated the demand motherhood would make on every aspect of my life was as obvious as a hole in the head. Not so apparent was the undue pressure I'd placed on teaching *literature* to validate me as a scholar. Teaching that particular course meant I had a right to be among those other smart people. It proved to the Ph.D.-carrying tutors that I was just as good as they were. It gave me a reason to finish my degree when I'd been running out of good reasons to do so. I had to teach it because, well, who would I be if not a professor? Now, the very people I'd hoped to impress knew that I was an imposter who didn't belong. And ... I still had to face my colleagues and pass those students in the cafeteria every. single. day.

I should've left after that, but I didn't. At the time I hadn't recognized it as yet another life-changing event inducing me to sever the final layer of umbilical cord that still held me to my mother as well as my youth. From somewhere deep inside me, I was being urged to cast aside the prescribed image of a strong, independent black woman and create a new one *in* my own terms and *on* my own terms. But I stayed. For years I'd witnessed my mother going back and forth to a job she despised because she had to. I stayed because of the lessons she'd drilled into me. If I left, I'd have to depend on Vinz financially, and she warned me never to do that.

"Make sure you have a savings account that he doesn't know anything about," she'd preached. "Even if it's just five dollars, you add to it every payday. That way, if he leaves, you'll have something to fall back on."

Her wise words had lingered all those years. To tell the truth, I stayed because I hadn't come up with my own wise words to replace hers. I didn't have the vocabulary to rebut the message that my hair wasn't straight enough, my skin light enough, my wallet full enough to be black. I couldn't articulate my most terrifying fear of not working: I'd become a white woman, and I couldn't have that.

As a child trying to visualize what I wanted to be when I grew up, a white housewife never even made the shortlist. On the contrary, I imagined myself single and supporting my kids on my executive's salary. In a few words – a strong, independent, black woman who didn't need anybody, not even the father of my children. After all, it was my birthright, handed down to me from my mother who'd inherited it from her mother and so on for generations.

I'd heard it said that we resist the very thing we need. How else would I explain the aversion I felt to Gwyneth Paltrow? She's Hollywood royalty born to distinguished parents who gave her every advantage that I never had. She adored her father, and he apparently adored her right back. She won an Oscar. People actually care about her current diet and exercise regime, for God's sake. And how the country grieved for her when she broke her engagement with Brad Pitt. (No one cared when my mother divorced my father.) It wasn't enough that she was in the movies or that her face was plastered on the cover of every other magazine in the bookstand. She had the nerve to show up in one of my poems. Each time I saw her blond hair and thin body I'd seethe, because she represented everything the white community told me I could never be and the black community taught me to despise.

How could I justify loathing someone who'd

never done me wrong? How could I hate an actress who is loved by so many? How could I have the slightest interest in reading her website, GOOP? (How do I even know the name of it?) I knew why ... I wanted what she had: recognition, legitimacy, privilege, the things I always felt were denied to me because I was a black woman. I never thought I was white, even though, for most of my life, I'd longed to be coddled, especially by my father. I'd yearned for someone to whisper, in my darkest hours, that everything was going to be all right. Shit, I knew only too well that I wasn't white; I knew I was destined to live a hard life working in the cotton fields of corporate America while Missy Ann just strolled to the top of the corporate ladder holding on to Daddy's hand for support, lest she miss a step and fall on her pretty little blond head.

When America looked at a white woman, say like Gwyneth Paltrow, it saw a cuddly creature that needed protection. She wasn't expected to work or over-exert herself with the demands of housework. Hell, she wasn't even expected to raise her kids by herself. White men wanted her, black men wanted her and black women wanted to be her. She set the standards of beauty. An entire toy empire had been modeled after the idealized white woman, and everyone knew how good Barbie's life was. Her lifestyle and life choices were validated in advertisements, in the media, on television and especially in Hollywood. Case in point was the motherhood vs. career woman debate that sparked my current dilemma. It was created by white scholars decades and decades ago after white women had entered the work force en masse. For centuries black women *were* the work force. For far too long black women ran white women's households and then went home to their own. Historically, black women in America had always combined motherhood and work. They had never had the luxury of a choice.

I didn't want to *be* Gwyneth Paltrow; I wanted what she represented. At the time, I believed that walking away from my career and focusing my energy on my new baby, running my household and supporting my husband's career was tantamount to trying to be white. Even worse, it was betraying the black sisterhood. What right did I have to put my feet up? What business did I have not choosing between paying the car note and the electric bill? My answer to those questions was to stay in a toxic work situation and, like my mother, hate every minute of it.

The scandal blew over at work, and I dedicated the following year to my advising duties.

I also stopped nursing Chloë, which added a physical boost to the emotional energy I'd been building. It was the ideal space in which to focus on finishing my dissertation. Although my committee's supervisor was enthusiastic about my project, I struggled to maintain my motivation. I was losing interest in my topic as well as my faith in literature as the best means for deconstructing the traditional image of the black female body. When I chose to spend time with my family or do anything other than read literary criticism, I felt guilty. Yet, I dreaded the hours I spent sitting alone with stacks of books and papers spread out around my desk at home spewing out what a hundred other scholars had already theorized about my topic. The dissertation had become a chore.

The only positive aspect was reconnecting with Tanya, who was born in Guyana and raised in the US. I'd met her during graduate school in a course on performance poetry of the Caribbean. I'd been struck by her intelligence and attracted to her eloquence. We'd kept in touch over the years, and when she told me she was writing her dissertation, I suggested we form our own little weekly support group. Calling her every Sunday was the backbone of my own dissertation-writing process. She was as resourceful as any library. She was support incarnate. She was my ticket back into the black community. We spent more time talking about our struggles and victories and our love lives and pet peeves than engaging in intellectual conversations about literary theory. She belied my mother's repeated warnings that black women would always be jealous of me.

But it wasn't enough. I'd been wavering between continuing with the Ph.D. program and dropping out. By the time I called my father to ask his advice, I'd already subconsciously made my decision and was hoping he'd talk me out of it. Boy, was I in for a surprise.

"You just had a baby, Little Carolyn," he informed me. "You have got to readjust your priorities."

"What if I make the wrong decision?" I prodded.

"You won't."

"But how do you know that for sure, Dad, when I'm not even sure what I want to do?" I shot back.

"Because every major decision you've made has turned out well. That's how I know that your decision to quit the program will be a good one."

After a few seconds of silence, he added, "You can always go back to school when Chloë's older."

The following week I emailed my supervisor that I was dropping out of the program. He tried to persuade me otherwise, but my mind was made up. I had no idea what I would do professionally, but the physical relief and emotional release I felt testified that I had made the right decision. Letting go of academia as the cornerstone of my identity freed up space in which to reflect and eventually rebuild. Most significantly, I started seeing myself with new eyes.

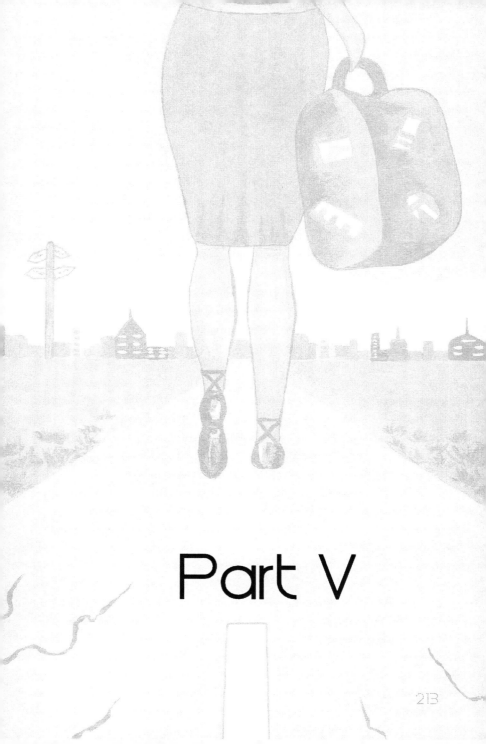

Part V

"Mijn mama is bruin," Chloë announced with pride to her little friend Maureen one afternoon when I was picking her up from daycare.

One of the teachers who'd also overheard Chloë's comment, replied, "Yes, that's right; your mama is brown. Is Chloë brown, too?"

Chloë held out her hand and looked at it before answering, "*Chloë is een beetje bruin.*"

Her teacher and I giggled. "Yes," I intervened, "Chloë's a little bit brown."

"And what about Papa?" the teacher pushed.

"There's not enough sun in Holland to make him brown," I whispered to the teacher between chuckles before Chloë informed us that her papa wasn't brown yet.

At three my child noticed these basic and simple differences between my body and her own. She couldn't quite connect all the dots, but she knew, at least on a biological level, that we were different. She was obviously trying to make heads or tails of this observation because that evening, as I was reading her a bedtime story, she asked me when she was going to turn brown.

Here was my first opportunity to begin a dialogue about race that differed from that which my mother had had with me. Here was my first stab at parenting Chloë as *me*, not as my mother parenting through me. I decided to treat it as pragmatically as Vinz had when Chloë had asked him where her penis was.

"You're not going to be brown, baby girl," I replied.

She insisted that when she got big, she would too turn brown, just like her mama. To lay the foundation for a future, healthy self-image, I told her, "Chloë, you're beautiful just as you are," which is what I'd needed to be told repeatedly from my parents, my community and my culture.

She seemed satisfied with that answer, and so was I. In the seven years I'd been living in Holland,

I'd come to discover that it was the ideal environment in which to remove race from my parenting because, unlike Americans, Dutch children are not raised with race. They don't learn to use it as a point of departure to explain or justify inequalities. It is not their point of reference in understanding history or economics or even politics. That's not to imply that racism and racial discrimination are absent from the Dutch mentality. But they do not shape their worldview. That they'd integrated people of African descent, at least on a small scale, was evidenced in things that might seem inconsequential to the casual eye but, for me, were impressive.

For example, Dutch television broadcast positive images of blacks that I'd never seen in America: a mixed couple (black woman, white man) inquiring about a mortgage, a black father cuddling his black baby tenderly in a commercial for baby lotion, a black woman advertising feminine hygiene products. Blacks were not depicted as stereotypes but as part of the Dutch community, participating in healthy relationships. They were not shown leading "black" lives; they were leading Dutch lives.

The America I grew up in disparaged black culture, relegating it to the margins of mainstream culture. Black Americans, including myself, internalized the message that we were of no consequence, mere outcasts trespassing on the American Dream. Dutch people, on the other hand, were curious about my black culture, taking a genuine interest in its particularities. Indeed, in the Dutch sensibility, nationality trumped race so that I was approaching a level of comfort and status that I'd never felt before. I felt safe enough to drop my guard and give myself permission to stop seeing the events of life exclusively through the lens of race, to stop looking for racism embedded in each comment and every gesture of a white person.

When Chloë and I were out and about, random white Dutch people would often approach us and exalt her corkscrew curls. I wasn't put off when I was asked if Chloë's father was a white Dutchman. That question was usually to place the fact that her hair was dirty blond, not dark brown like mine, and her skin fair. Not once did that question carry an undertone of the hardships my interracial daughter would probably endure. Instead of leading to subtle disapproval, the question of Vinz's race and nationality cued approval once the conversation turned to our raising her in a bilingual household. The Dutch revere multilingualism, in part because very few countries outside of Holland speak their language. They seem to have inherited a collective wanderlust from their merchant forefathers because I'd never come across a people that value travel as much as the Dutch do. They're convinced of the advantages of being raised bilingual, and the idea of a daughter of mine being advantaged is appealing.

Taking that emphasis off race allowed me to reevaluate my own politics. I had bought into the one-drop rule, a racist tenet that deems any person with a black ancestor, no matter how far back, to be black. I'd explained that to Vinz when he'd asked me why I referred to Chloë as a black girl.

"She's also Dutch, you know," he rebutted.

"When she goes to America, she'll be seen as a black girl," I retorted.

"But she's being raised in Holland," he argued.

"You don't understand because you're not black," I bantered.

"No, but I do understand that black people can be too quick to make assumptions."

Then he proceeded to remind me of his years working in the hotel industry in D.C. and New Orleans.

"The black employees saw a white man in a managerial position, and that automatically made me a racist. They only warmed up to me when they saw me with you. I don't want my daughter to learn that."

His persuasive arguments put me in a quandary. On the one hand, I felt the need to prepare her for the racism she was bound to encounter. Much like my mother had tried to prepare me. On the other hand, I agreed with Vinz that we should raise Chloë to judge others on their individual actions and not hold individuals accountable for the actions of the group. In turn, we would teach her to expect the same from others. In a perfect world, reciprocity would rule. Unfortunately, our world is deadly to those who hide their head in the sand.

I wanted her to experience soul food and feel soul music in her body's every organ. I wanted to teach her how to move her hips and bob her head when she danced. I wanted her to discover her own rhythm and to notice it in the words she'll choose or in the way she'll walk through life, bringing color to those around her. I wanted her to know about our struggle for equality in America and that, in many ways, that war hasn't been won. I wanted eventually to engage her in dialogue about what she might contribute to the battle. I wanted her to hug her black American heritage as tightly as she would the Dutch/European legacy running through her veins.

In the end we agreed that we would not divide our focus or politicize her identity by focusing on black/white, Dutch/American. Rather, we'd join forces to equip her with a strong sense of self that is not dependent upon what she looks like. If we got our way, her sense of worth would be impenetrable to those who would shun her because her daddy's white. Her self-image would be impervious to anyone telling a racist joke, unaware that she has a black mama. Her sense of self would deflect any challenge to her national authenticity because her mama speaks Dutch with an accent.

Free from the constraints of being judged purely on racial terms, I could explore other aspects of my life, like doing *fun* things with Chloë. I stumbled upon a mother-and-tot music class, given in English. With Chloë in a baby seat mounted on my handlebars, I cycled to the train station in Voorschoten, took the train to The Hague, during rush hour, got on the tram and then walked a couple of blocks to the class. Not once did I wonder if I was going to be the only black person in that class. Instead, I thought about where the other mothers might come from. I got excited about the possibility of making playdates with other children. I felt enthusiastic about this acclaimed international program that introduced young children to classical music in a fun way. We would be singing and dancing to songs and lullabies from around the world as well as playing various instruments.

When I walked into the class that first day, I was tickled to see that the instructor was Latina with long, dark wavy hair, big brown eyes and skin a shade darker than mine. She hailed from the Dominican Republic but had studied music in America where she'd also been a concert pianist before marrying a Dutchman and immigrating to Holland. I was thrilled that Chloë would be interacting with another brown-skinned person besides her mother.

Then a lady walked in with her toddler, who was about a year younger than Chloë. She had the smoothest dark skin and the loveliest dimples I'd always longed for. I never understood why both my sisters were blessed with dimples and I wasn't. Though dressed casually, this lady's clothes were obviously as expensive as they were pretty and stylish. I felt envy creeping up my neck and was reminded of my habitual reaction to meeting people with money, since I grew up with so little. But, my need to connect with another black woman was more urgent than my inferiority complex, so I made eye contact with her and found that she was as happy to meet me as I was to meet her. She and her little girl sat on the floor next to Chloë and me.

After class we chatted, and I found out her name was Monique. Over the following few weeks we saw each other in the music class and chatted for a while afterwards. We eventually met up for lunch, where I found out that we had more in common than just living in Holland. She grew up in California but decided to get her undergraduate degree from Notre Dame in South Bend, Indiana. From there she moved to Washington, D.C., where she got a law degree from Howard and married the man of her dreams, also a Howard law student and a white man.

Over a bottle of fizzy water and a *broodje croquette*, veal croquette sandwich, I asked her how they, two Americans, ended up in Holland.

"An opportunity presented itself, and we took it," she explained as she ate her salad.

Her husband had been offered a position in the legal department of an international telecommunications company. They'd been in Holland about as long as I had, about seven years. She explained that they'd spent the first years traveling around Europe until they had their first daughter.

I cut to the chase and asked, "Has your experience as a black woman been any different in Holland than in America?"

She put her knife and fork side by side on the plate, which is the European way of showing that you're done eating, and replied thoughtfully, "Going with my husband, for example, to work-related events, I'm almost always the only black person there, and I'm always self-conscious about it, where I don't think that Dutch people approach it like that."

She continued, "Maybe in the US they would think 'Oh there's a black person', but here I don't think they do, and I don't think that I've embraced that yet. I'm not letting myself just be free in that... does that make sense?"

The waiter taking away her empty plate seemed to free up space for her to continue her reflections.

"It might make going back to America easier. If you're not holding on to race so hard. Then it might open more doors, give you more opportunities."

"Mmm hmm, you got that right," I replied.

"I also think, with respect to my children, when we're permanently in the States, they can mark more than one box because they're biracial. We're finally getting past the one-drop rule, and if I'm more open, free about race and blackness then I won't push that on them, and they'll be more free to be who they are."

Those words were music to my ears. Sitting in a small café in the *Staten Kwartier* in The Hague, Monique had just validated my parenting plan of erasing the boundaries that America the racialized has drawn around our lives. Sadly, those boundaries had stifled me to the extent that I expatriated. I wondered how many other black American women felt stifled by the old racial etiquette?

So I asked her, sipping a now lukewarm cup of *rooibos* tea. "Do you think things have really changed in America?"

A flash of regret in her eyes told me her answer before she spoke.

"I don't know," she replied. "When I grew up, I was accused of thinking I was white because of the way I spoke, because I went to school, got educated and did different things. I didn't want to feel like I was turning my back on the race or betraying anybody. Those are things that are still on my mind, unfortunately."

She continued.

"I remember when my oldest daughter was very little, and my nephew, who's probably about my complexion, said something about her white skin. I thought about the things my kids get to do, the opportunities they have. I think people associate it with the fact that I'm married to a white man. I find myself thinking that I'm black, they're half-black. I always want to put it back to that. People think my life is 'like that' just because my husband is white."

What started as a connection based solely on our brown skin ended up being much deeper than that. It wasn't just my mother who had passed along her version of race. Monique's comments made me realize that, yes, the black community had been hard at work to ensure that we kept up the image of hard work and sacrifice. Indeed, our mothers and grandmothers and great-grandmothers literally worked their fingers to the bone because they had to. America gave them no other choice. The black community gave them no other choice. If we didn't choose that same route, we were sell-outs. We felt guilty for living a good life.

We paid the bill and started gathering our things. Before we went our separate ways, I decided to invite her and her family to celebrate *Sinterklaas* with us. Her smooth forehead crinkled briefly in thought before she asked, a bit tentatively, "Are there any pictures of Black Pete in your house?"

I smiled, knowing that I had a comrade in Monique, and replied, "I've already made it clear to Vinz that I'll never allow Black Pete in my house."

"In that case, when should we be there?"

Sinterklaas, celebrated on the fifth of December, has many parallels with Christmas, though for the average Dutch person, *Sinterklaas* is unthinkable without Black Pete dressed up in medieval Turkish or Moorish costume, black curly wig, face painted with thick black paint, and bright red lipstick, skipping about and tossing treats to the little ones. The average Dutch person sees no harm in Black Pete and insists that there is no racist undertone. When I'd first come to Holland, I'd gone with Vinz and his mother to watch the *Sinterklaas* festivities in downtown Goes. Vinz suddenly turned to me and gave me a handful of *peppernoten*, tiny spiced cookies that are all the rage during that time of year.

"I don't want any," I said.

"They're not for you," he explained. "You give them out to the kids when they come over to you."

"Huh?"

Then Vinz looked at my curly hair exploding out from under the black beret I wore at the time and giggled.

"What's so funny?" I'd asked.

"Black Pete also wears a beret."

"That's not funny, Vinz," I'd said.

"I'm sorry," he said upon seeing my serious expression. "I didn't mean to offend you," he apologized.

For the average American living in Holland, images of Black Pete adorning wrapping paper or decorating shop windows is a reminder of a disturbing period in American history. Later on that day, I'd explained to Vinz that Black Pete is little more than blackface.

"It's just a part of Dutch culture, Carolyn," he'd claimed. "We're not making fun of black people."

"Ok, but why do people have to paint their faces coal black?"

"Because he climbs down the fireplace to stuff goodies in kids' shoes. Have you ever been in a chimney?" he'd asked smugly. "Obviously not, because otherwise you'd know that soot sticks to your face. That's why he's called Black Pete."

"I get that. But why can't they smear a little bit of gray on their cheeks? And what about the bright red lipstick?"

He hadn't had an answer to that one.

Then I got up on my soapbox.

"Do you know what blackface minstrelsy is?" I'd asked him. "Well, white performers would paint their faces coal black, smear on bright red lipstick and don the clothes that black slaves wore. On stage these performers would copy the slaves' movements, music and the way they talked. But they made it seem like blacks were child-like fools. It was a caricature of black people. Those shows just reaffirmed what white society thought of blacks anyway."

That's why I'd found Black Pete so offensive.

Children in particular loved to run around in their little Black Pete get up, and I'd dreaded when Chloë would ask if she could have a Black Pete costume. She was three and still hadn't asked. Ironically, over the years my indignation had waned. While I hadn't quite let go of all my American racial baggage, I could broaden the context to include considering how the Dutch culture interacted with race on a daily basis, instead of focusing on the holiday exclusively through the lens of American-based racism.

I couldn't dismiss the fact that Vinz had brought home a black woman . . . a foreign one at that. His family and friends had accepted me and our relationship from day one. Even before we'd had plans to marry, his parents would introduce me to their friends as their daughter-in-law, not as their son's girlfriend. On top of that, I'd regularly seen white Dutch men with their black (African, American, Indonesian, Caribbean) girlfriends, wives and children. I'd not seen as many mixed couples in America as I'd seen in the short time I'd been in Holland. When I considered the positive images of blacks I'd seen on television and the warmth with which I'd been received in general, I was hard pressed to assign racist intentions to Black Pete.

Of course, I couldn't ignore Dutch history, either. They could not have colonized the East Indies nor enslaved the West Indies (Suriname, Curacao, Bonaire, St. Eustatius, St. Maarten, Saba and Aruba) without employing a hefty racist ideology to justify their presence. Many Dutch people were quick to deny their ancestors' role as the oppressor, which I'd found unsettling, at the very least. Rationalizations abounded, such as Dutch slave owners not being as cruel as the Spanish or their not being involved with the slave trade as long as the French or that Dutch slavers hadn't shipped as many Africans as the English. Dutch people themselves had admitted that their educational system, formal and informal, had glossed over Dutch colonial history.

However, the gravest problem I could see was that the Dutch didn't question their country's involvement in the colonization of Asia and America and the enslavement of Africans, just as they did not question Black Pete, even amidst the reproach he inspired. In my opinion Black Pete would be an ideal starting point for the Dutch to engage their racial politics.

Although Monique and her mixed, multicultural family celebrated a Black-Pete-free holiday with us, we would go our separate ways for years, until our paths met up again. If my mother had been wrong in her admonishments that dark-skinned black women would not like me, which other of her realities did I have to dismantle on my road to creating my own image of black womanhood? Luckily, plenty of positive black women began crossing my path to help me with my reintegration process. I started running into sisters left and right. Like on the tram in The Hague one afternoon when I was on my way home from the American Book Center.

I'd heard her talking on her cell phone and knew from her accent that she was American. Her conversation finished, I turned around and asked her which state she was from. We chatted about all the delights of living abroad that can be squeezed into a ten-minute tram ride. When the tram stopped at *Centraal Station* I stepped off, said goodbye and headed for my train.

"Excuse me," said a slightly breathless voice behind me. I turned around to the black woman I'd just met. I stopped and waited for her to catch up. "Can I ask you something?"

"Yes, of course," I said, checking my watch to make sure I actually had time to chat before my train left.

"Where do you get your hair done?"

We exchanged telephone numbers and met once for lunch before she moved to England.

*A*fter years of home-relaxing my hair and having it cut twice a year, when my sister-in-law Lyan so graciously took time away from her active family life to do so, I stumbled upon a beauty shop, a hop, skip and a jump from my front door. I literally stumbled upon it. I was shopping downtown in Leiden, and I tripped over an annoying cobblestone that the Dutch are so fond of. My heart melted at the hot-pink-streaked wigs and the cobalt-blue-highlighted culture braids on display at "Rita's". I walked in and gasped at all the boxes of Dark & Lovely this and Pink that, mixed in with a little Crème of Nature. There was enough product there to rival any Sally's Beauty Supply . . . well . . . on a much smaller scale, of course.

For months I'd buy my products from the small West African woman who visited the States several times a year to "keep updated", as Rita explained. I'd finally had enough of walking around with my hair all over my head, and as this was the period before the reemergence of the Afro and the popularity of sister locks, I asked Rita if she could relax my hair.

She was in the middle of trimming a male customer's hair, but that didn't stop her from running her stubby fingers through my hair, just like the beauticians in America did, and informing me that my hair needed deep conditioning.

"I relax your hair. Then I give you condition," she began. "I use herbs from Africa. Good?"

It was all good. Where in America had I ever had the opportunity to have my hair brought back to life by herbs straight from the Mother Country? And being from West Africa, Rita oozed an authenticity that I'd been longing for. My eyes met those of her customer in the mirror above her workstation that contained a blow dryer, some rollers and various cans of hairspray. He was obviously piqued that Rita had turned her attention from his fade.

Cutting to the chase, I asked, "How much will it cost?"

"I use herbs from Africa. It will cost 115 euros."

Ridiculous, I thought. I'd never paid more than $65 in the States. On the other hand, I needed to get my hair done. We were in Holland, so those products must have been expensive to import. And I *was* intrigued by that deep conditioner. Things were always more expensive overseas, so what the hell, I concluded.

"When can you do it?"

"I do right now," she started, but was cut off by her male customer's oh-no-you-didn't-look. "When I finish."

I took a seat at the only hair dryer in the back of the store, where she did hair. I looked around the shop, taking in the dingy walls and the lack of customers. My gaze rested on Rita. Was she clipping that man's hair faster than before? Did she cut him off when he asked her a question? Was she trying to get him out of the chair as fast as she could? I continued my visual tour around to the hairpieces of varying lengths, colors and textures, to the small display of bright eye shadow and mahogany lipstick.

I recalled the years before I graduated from high school, when my mother and I had gone to our beauty shop, The Perfect Touch, every other Saturday after she'd gotten paid. Every other Saturday I'd see the same women having their hair set on rollers and sitting under the same dryer as the time before. I'd smell the same scorched hair of the same children folding down the tops of their ears lest they be scalded by the straightening comb. The hairdressers had animated the stories they'd watched the week before.

"Ain't Erica Kane a trip?" one of them would say, followed by a chorus of "I wish she would try to take my man" and indignant laughter. In the background WTLC, the only soul radio station in Indianapolis back then, kept us grooving and bobbing our heads to the beat of the latest hits, snapping our fingers.

The beauty shop had been an unspoken sisterhood: there were no white women, and the only men who entered the shop were selling fish platters. We'd spend all morning sitting there, mostly *waiting* to get our hair done, but I didn't mind. Although we the customers didn't talk amongst ourselves, there had been an energy of mutual understanding that had bordered on the intimate. Where else but the beauty shop could you go and see a bunch of black women willing to reveal their best-kept secret? Social status, skin color and hair texture didn't matter. We were all there because our hair was dirty, nappy and needed to be done.

Rita's offering me to sit down in the chair that had been occupied by her customer snapped me back to the stark landscape of her one-woman show in Holland. She fastened the plastic cape around my neck, and just as she was about to apply the relaxer, a young white girl with dreadlocks walked in and asked Rita if she had an ointment or oil for her hair.

"I don't know. You come back later. I look for you," said Rita as she walked back to where I sat.

After she applied the relaxer, she led me over to the sink where she washed it out, shampooed my hair, rinsed it and then walked over to what looked like a kitchen counter and cabinet. She had her back to me, so all I saw were her elbows reaching for this jar and pouring something from that bottle into it. Oooohhh, the conditioner, I thought. I could almost hear the drums beating.

I tried to look around her back to see what she was doing, but I didn't manage. She walked back to me and started applying the conditioner. It smelled familiar. I would have sworn it was Dark & Lovely, which I'd used throughout the years, but I could have been wrong. And what about the African herbs? I didn't smell anything out of the ordinary. Then, after she'd coated every strand of my hair, she asked me to lean my head back so she could rinse it out. Where was the plastic cap? Those herbs must have been so potent the conditioner didn't need fifteen minutes of dryer time to absorb into my roots. She proceeded to blow dry and then cut my hair. It didn't look any shinier or healthier than it had before, but then again, maybe those herbs were about strengthening my hair follicles. She finished and said, "150 euros please."

"Excuse me?"

"Yes, 150 euros please."

"You told me it would be one *fifteen*."

"No, I say one *fifty*. Plus twenty euros for the haircut."

Then it all hit me. That's why she couldn't wait to get that man out of her chair. She was afraid I'd change my mind. No wonder she didn't have time to look for a ten-euro bottle of dreadlock juice. She'd just found a fool and knocked her in the head. I refused to pay extra for the haircut, but I went ahead and paid one hundred and fifty euros for a friggin' relaxer. When I told Vinz about it later on that day, he studied my hair, asking me to turn around so he could check out the back.

"What did she do?"

I gave him my most menacing death look.

"She did charge you in guilders, right?" (which would have equaled seventy-five euros). He burst out laughing when I rolled my eyes and walked away.

Black women in America are raised to believe that the texture of our hair gives us our identity. The longer and straighter the hair, the higher the worth. Our hair politics relegate dark-skinned women with short, nappy hair to the bottom rung of the social, professional and even romantic ladder. What black person wasn't taught that the field slaves were the ones with the most African features: dark skin, broad noses, thick lips? What black person didn't know that the field slaves toiled under the scorching sun and the overseer's whip? Too bad that history lesson had left out what it really meant to be a house slave. Maybe then those external accidents of biology wouldn't have had such an enduring and calamitous influence on our intrinsic value. If those women were light-skinned, it was because their mothers had been raped by massa. Maybe their soft, delicate skin had been protected from the sun's harmful rays – and the sting of the whip – but their hides had had no protection from the mistress's abuse at knowing that her husband preferred violating a mere slave over making love with her. Their innocence had been ravaged by any male relative, acquaintance or bill collector who'd called in on the Big House. So who'd had it worse?

It took that experience at Rita's, where I'd paid 150 euros to get my hair relaxed, for me to realize that I'd bought into all those whack messages. I'd been miserable the first few years living in Holland, which must be the worst place on the planet for a black woman's hair. It's rainy and humid with a few dry, sunny weeks freckled here and there on the calendar. I didn't have a car, so my bike was my main transportation. On many occasion, I'd cycle away from my house under dry skies only to arrive at my destination wet, my hair puffed up in a 'fro. Funny, it *never* seemed to rain when I was on my way *back* home. I'd gotten tired of devoting hours to straightening my hair only to walk outside and have it frizz up. Whenever I wore my natural curls, I'd recall the time Vinz and I were listening to a jazz band in New Orleans. I couldn't help commenting to Vinz on the lead singer's attire: a bright red suit and white patent leather shoes. "And, he's got a Jheri Kurl," I'd said to Vinz, scarcely hiding my disgust. Vinz had looked at my hair and asked, "Isn't that what you have?"

I was tired of hating my hair. I was sick and tired of hating a vital part of my *self*. Throughout my life, I'd used my hair to show the world what I was experiencing in my own life. Growing up, I'd wanted to please my mother, so I'd spent most Saturdays in the beauty shop. If I couldn't lighten my skin, I sure could straighten my hair. In college my hair had become an unwilling accomplice to my cultural sabotage. I'd let my hair go wild just to spite the black community. Friends would chide me for not investing time and money into styling my hair. "Girl, you ain't white," I'd heard more than once. Little did those ladies know, by not doing my hair, I'd initiated a full-blown rebellion against our unwritten hair laws.

The years after graduating from college, I'd gotten used to my hair looking wild, unkempt and just plain uncombed. I thought that it was my way of telling the world that I didn't care what it thought of me, but actually I'd been giving others the power to interpret my meaning and then decide who I was. Refusing to put time and energy into something as mundane as doing my hair wasn't noble; my uncoiffed do simply said that I didn't care what I thought about myself.

By refusing to look at myself in the mirror, which I was still reluctant to do, I'd been putting an awful lot of energy into refusing to see myself. I'd been refusing to see my *self* as a beautiful person in spite of - and because of - my nappy/curly thick luscious hair . . . and brown skin. Truth was, I'd gotten tired of battling myself and started wondering what would happen if I took the focus off my hair. What would happen if I accepted my hair? If I could see my hair as just another appendage, with no more significance placed on it than I placed on my right arm or left leg, would I start to change how I saw my whole self in the world? And hadn't my new world pointed out to me just how beautiful my locks were? Whether I wore natural curls or relaxed curls, braids, short, long or straight hair, my Dutch friends and family constantly complimented it.

How could I so casually disparage any part of this body that had taken me all over the world, that, at thirty-eight, still looked fit and was healthy. Every cell of that body had participated in the creation and nurturing of Chloë, and I needed to acknowledge and celebrate that. How I treated my hair, as an extension of my body, directly reflected upon how I treated myself. I was in a position that empowered me to define myself on my terms rather than on those of the billion-dollar beauty industry, Hollywood or an obsolete racial doctrine that strived to dictate what I should aspire to look like.

It was only fitting that my hair, the very obstacle I would have used to stop me from moving to Holland with Vinz, had helped me reconnect to a vital part of myself. Indirectly, it had helped me reconnect with other black women abroad. Through my hair I had reconnected with myself, the one I wanted to show my daughter, the one who understood that I was not a mini-version of someone else's ideal but a force to be reckoned with.

Part VI

"You ain't gettin' no younger, girl," ticked the voice of my biological clock. *"If you want another baby, do it now."*

My master plan had always included having more than one child; however, my strategy had been to achieve professional success first. I was already thirty-eight and miserable at the university. By this time, I'd reckoned that the senior tutor's prediction that I'd ruined my career had come to pass. Not only was I not asked to teach another course, my advising duties had stagnated. New positions and projects bypassed me. Being honest with myself, I would admit that this situation was two-sided. I'd lost my passion for trying to equip my students with enough resources to enter the professional market after graduation. Academia no longer interested me. Besides, I'd grown tired of the long commute. I could always find another job; I wouldn't always be able to have a baby. So, leaving my job to have another baby should have been easy.

True, Vinz and I did depend on my steady paycheck. Each year I got a raise, paid maternity leave, five weeks of vacation, vacation money and a pension plan. I had financial security. And I had status. Where else was I going to find a sixteen-hour-per-week job that paid me close to twenty-five thousand euros a year to use my brain in an intellectually stimulating atmosphere? Plus, if I left the work force for a year or two to have a baby, would I return at the same level? I couldn't accept a new job and then, a few months later, get pregnant and leave for three months. Given my age, I wasn't willing to wait two or three years while I proved my worth in a new position. Ultimately, Vinz and I found a simple solution to this complicated problem: we'd go with whichever came first, a new job or a baby.

Nature won.

From day one of the pregnancy, which was exactly one month after I'd gotten off the pill, I was uneasy about it. I couldn't get the feeling out of my heart that I was going to miscarry, which was why I agreed to prenatal testing. Because of my age,

I'd learned, the risk of having a baby with Down syndrome dramatically increased. The results of a simple blood test showed that the chances were low for that condition. With that good news, Vinz and I went ahead with our ski vacation. Once I got on the slopes, that feeling of dread overcame me, and I lost my nerve. I returned my skis the next day and spent the rest of the week watching Austrian television. By the time we drove back to Holland, I'd made it past the first trimester and relaxed for the first time.

Around week twenty of the pregnancy, my midwife recommended I take advantage of a new program in Holland that allowed for a midterm ultrasound. I initially declined, dismissing it as her paranoia at my "at risk" pregnancy. But then my midwife explained that she recommended it to all of her clients, regardless of age because, if there were a problem, like a heart condition or kidney disease, it might be caught early enough to take appropriate steps to care for the baby as soon as it was born. It sounded reasonable enough to me. Plus, I was curious about the baby's gender, so I agreed.

Nothing prepared me for what the obstetrician saw. Or didn't see, as the case was. One of the baby's kidneys was missing, the baby's heart was severely underdeveloped. The legs were too thin and one foot was clubbed. An immediate amniocentesis confirmed the obstetrician's diagnosis of trisomy 13, a genetic condition that caused severe physical deformation and mental retardation. He explained that it had nothing to do with my age. Statistically, it had to happen to someone's baby; unfortunately, it happened to ours.

Vinz and I thought about carrying on with the pregnancy, but the obstetrician assured us that no babies with trisomy 13 lived outside the womb longer than a few weeks. Because my pregnancy had advanced to the second trimester, I would have to go through the birthing process and deliver a stillborn baby. The following week Vinz and I searched our individual souls for an answer to our question: what was the most compassionate decision for our baby as well as our little family? We decided to stop the pregnancy, and on March 22, 2006, Jesse van Es was born. She'd died as peacefully as she'd lived, loved and protected in my womb.

Shortly after holding our baby girl and then saying goodbye to her, I was told that I'd need to go to the OR to have the placenta scraped from my body. As I was being wheeled to the elevator, the most beautiful and miraculous thing happened. A door to one of the birthing rooms opened, and a father came out, holding his newborn baby. Amidst profuse apologies from the hospital staff, my eyes met Vinz's in a brief glimpse of mutual understanding. About a week later, after I'd recovered physically, Vinz and I discussed that moment and discovered we'd had the same thought: life goes on. Our baby may have died, but another was born. We could either stand still with death or move on with life. We chose to live.

Without understanding why, I cried incessantly for the first two weeks. After all, I never knew Jesse and had no memories of her to treasure. My midwife came by one afternoon and talked to me for hours. I told her about my uneasiness during the pregnancy, and she concluded that perhaps on a subconscious level I'd known that Jesse and I had but a short time together and had already bonded with her. She urged me to cry, and I did. Besides Vinz, the only other person I could bear to see or speak with was my mother. She was the one person who knew what I was going through. She understood why I didn't have the energy right then to pay attention to Chloë. In turn I understood why she hadn't been able to show me a lot of affection after losing Dawn. Although I was thousands of miles away from her, I felt as close to my mother as she'd felt to Grandma Thelma, sitting a few feet from her, when Cory had died.

Early on in my grieving process I decided to keep reminding myself of all the gifts that had been bestowed upon me, upon us. I didn't have the healthy, bubbly baby girl I'd had my heart set on. But I did have Chloë, and when I cuddled with her, I thanked the universe for entrusting her to us. Instead of shutting down, Vinz actually talked to me at length about his emotions, acknowledging how grateful he was to have held Jesse. He hadn't planned on even taking pictures of her, and now he had a loving image of his second-born daughter forever imprinted on his heart. Words of love and support came pouring in from friends and family from all over the world. The colleagues who'd shown me little sympathy after the birth of my first child, sent emails filled with compassion after the death of my second one. I looked around my house and found gifts in every piece of second-hand furniture that Vinz's family had given us when we'd had nothing. I knew I'd been blessed. Jesse had spent her entire life with me, with *me*, and how many parents had ever received such a divine gift?

*H*olland is a country in which workers have rights, and the university administration informed me that I was entitled to at least sixteen weeks of paid leave, the same amount of maternity leave I would have taken. The only condition was that I consult the university psychologist. At the end of my first appointment, two months after losing Jesse, the psychologist not only suggested I take the full sixteen weeks to recover, she recommended that Vinz and I take Chloë and go somewhere for a couple of weeks. Maybe a change of scenery would ease the grieving process. We did more than change the scenery: we changed continents.

One of Vinz's buddies from the hotel school and his Brazilian wife had just bought a house in Brazil. Vincent and Renata had been urging us to come visit, and we had the perfect excuse to be decadent, so we booked our tickets. Unfortunately, our little getaway got off to a rocky start. The Saturday before we were scheduled to fly, I'd googled the weather forecast for the São Paulo region. I stumbled upon a link that informed me that, as an American, I needed a visa.

"No you don't," Vinz contradicted the internet after I'd passed along the information. "Vincent already checked into it and told me we didn't need one flying from Holland."

"Why don't you call Vincent and double check."

Sure enough, people flying from Holland *with a Dutch passport* didn't need a visa to enter Brazil. Vincent assumed I had one. Since I didn't, I'd have to wait until Monday, the day before we were scheduled to fly, to travel to the Brazilian consulate in Rotterdam and arrange an expedited visa. I wasn't worried about spending an extra hundred euros to get away and take our minds off losing our baby, if only for two weeks. Good thing I wasn't worried about the paltry fee to expedite the visa process because we'd end up paying *eight hundred* euros to buy a new ticket.

The bureaucrat who "helped" me refused to bend the forty-eight-hour visa-processing policy. He denied the existence of an expedited visa. I spent the entire day at the consulate. Several of Vinz's hotel school friends worked for KLM Royal Dutch airline, but not one of them could work around the bureaucrat's ruling. I had no option but to drive Chloë and Vinz to Schiphol airport the next day, pick up my visa the day after and fly out on Wednesday.

Ubatuba, the land of many canoes, was worth every moment of the visa fiasco. Our friends' spacious, three-story house was built into the side of a mountain overlooking the ocean. The house was equipped with a brick pizza oven and bar area next to their private swimming pool. Chloë, Vinz and I had the entire bottom floor to ourselves. The house's most captivating feature was the sound of waves breaking the surface that coaxed me out of my slumber each morning and lulled me back to sleep at night.

We found out that Ubatuba boasted over seventy beaches, and we set out to visit each one. While they weren't always maintained, they were virtually empty as it was May, late fall, and most of the tourists and vacation-home owners had already vacated the area. There were enough people, however, for me to notice the prevalence of thong bikinis. Brazilian women of all shapes, sizes and ages were sporting them, and the smaller the better. Renata insisted I buy one, pooh-poohing away my self-consciousness about my mushy post-partum body. I ended up buying two.

We spent most mornings and early afternoons lying on a beach somewhere. Afterwards, we'd go back to the house for a cocktail or two, usually a *caipirinha* made with fresh-squeezed lime juice, sugar and *cachaça*, or *pinga*, as it's called there, poured over crushed ice. Most evenings we'd drive into town for dinner. At one restaurant we helped ourselves to the most appetizing buffet of side dishes: beans, rice, cassava, pasta and local veggies. A waiter regularly wheeled a cart of various grilled, baked or fried meats, which were cut and served to us at our table. The other evenings Renata showed off her culinary skills. There was nothing she couldn't prepare: fish and seafood, meat, pizza. She made the most sumptuous *feijouada*, Brazil's national dish of black beans, rice and sausage.

Besides being the perfect hosts, Vincent and Renate were the perfect friends, gracious and compassionate. They listened to our story with tears in their eyes and entertained us enough to laugh away ours. They gave us our space as willingly as giving us their time. I started seeing myself with different eyes. I was no longer the poor girl with the traumatic past; I'd grown into a cosmopolitan woman with the means to escape the pain of loss for a couple of weeks in a part of the world I'd never have considered had it not been for my expanded circle of friends. I wasn't bitter nor was I mad about what had recently happened nor about what I'd survived.

Losing baby Jesse had taught me that life was short and that there were some things that I had absolutely no control over. I couldn't control what had already happened in my past. I had no control over what people thought of me. But, what did I have control over? I realized that I could determine the extent to which I *let* losing my baby affect me. I realized that I could determine the extent to which I *let* the tragedies of my childhood affect me. I realized I could determine how I spent my days.

"Well I'll be damned," whispered my voice.

"No, I won't be damned," I said aloud, taking inspiration from Barbra Streisand's character Fanny Brice in *Funny Lady* when she'd finally let go of loving Nicky Arnstein as the thing that defined her identity.

Working at a job that I'd grown to hate had been determining the course of my days for way too long. Ironically, while sunbathing on one of our private beaches, far away from the university, I finally acknowledged the distaste I felt at the very thought of going back to that place that I had let determine my outlook on life. Even when I was off, I'd spend precious moments dreading the long commute to a job that was leading me nowhere. Advising students on which courses they needed to take to graduate no longer fulfilled me. Spending hours in faculty meetings and on pointless project assignments was tedious, to say the least. I'd felt disconnected from my colleagues and had started eating lunch at my desk instead of in the dining hall with them.

Moreover, I was bored, and when I looked into the heart of that boredom I saw that I was capable of doing so much more. I'd been itching to tap into my potential. The only problem was that I didn't know what that potential was, which allowed that question to pop back up: who would I be if not an academic? This time, though, I refused to let fear dictate the answer. I'd just survived one of the biggest fears of my life: losing a child. I resolved to arm myself with courage and entertain a different answer. I would leave academia. It was only a question of when.

Three months after returning from Brazil I got pregnant. I also got the answer to the question of when I'd leave the university, which was at the end of my maternity leave. The only thing between me and putting my plan into action was nine long months. On the other hand, I'd have nine long months to create a plan because I had no idea what I'd do once I quit my job. As it went, having an end in sight only increased my restlessness. Every time I crossed off a day, I sent up a silent prayer that the universe would create a new university policy that would grant me an additional four months of paid maternity leave that

I could take before the baby was born. The universe didn't send me a new policy, but it did send me a yeast infection from hell.

It also initiated me into a side of Dutch gynecology and obstetrics that I hadn't experienced before because Chloë's pregnancy had been so smooth. Carrying Chloë had been like creating a classical text on the beauty of pregnancy. I'd felt so good it was borderline sickening even though I never suffered from one morning of nausea. My weirdest craving had been for fruit. I couldn't eat enough bananas, melons or berries. I'd felt good and looked even better. I'd been all stomach, so from behind it had been impossible to tell I was pregnant, even at thirty weeks. I'd cycled to the train station up until my maternity leave. My only difficulty had been managing the urgent impatience to meet the sweet little being growing inside me.

The yeast growing inside me at the beginning of this my third pregnancy sent me straight to my GP, who was unable to prescribe me anything stronger than a topical cream that did little more than irritate me because it didn't work. I went back *a few weeks later* only to be given a prescription for a suppository that may have worked better than the cream, but it still didn't take away the itch.

I could appreciate her explanation that stronger medications were not advised during the first trimester seeing as no studies had been done on the possible affects on a fetus. And, she assured me that *candida* would not affect its development.

"It's annoying but not life threatening," she said. True, a yeast infection wasn't life threatening for me or for my baby, but it wasn't merely irritating, it was downright frustrating because I couldn't scratch in public. So, I waited.

Toward the end of the first trimester – yes, I had a yeast infection for three months – I decided to take things into my own hands, literally. I'd always heard that the bacteria in yoghurt was an effective, natural way to cure a yeast infection, so I went to the grocery store and bought the thickest yoghurt I could find along with a pair of thin latex gloves and was ready to get to work.

I'd been self-ministering my condition a day or two before the unthinkable happened: I started bleeding one evening after my pre-bedtime dosage of yoghurt. My heart sank just before I started yelling for Vinz to call the midwife because I was miscarrying.

My midwife had been having dinner with friends when she got me on the line and went through her retinue of questions. She didn't seem too concerned when she found out what I was doing prior to the bleeding but offered to swing by to examine me. Within fifteen minutes she was at our house taking my blood pressure and pressing on my lower abdomen. She then asked to see my hands.

"Why do you need to look at my hands?"

"I want to see your nails," she replied.

The confusion on my face prompted her lesson in reproductive biology. "When you're pregnant, the skin on the cervix becomes thin. The blood vessels are closer to the surface and are more vulnerable. I think your long nail opened up a blood vessel."

"So I'm not miscarrying?" I confirmed.

"No. But I'll give you a few syringes for the yoghurt."

Self-help be damned. I went back to my GP and suggested she do a pap smear to make sure it wasn't anything more serious than a yeast infection. I'd never been pregnant in America, but I sensed that a pap smear would have been the first course of action had I been. I had little doubt that an American doctor would have probably nuked it all before letting me suffer for months, yet there I was, telling a Dutch doctor that I needed to be examined "down there".

She sent me to a (male) gynecologist. He turned his back while I took off my pants and underwear and lay down on the examining table. I didn't get a robe or even a sheet. He took one look at my vulva – he didn't touch it, mind you, let alone use a speculum to actually look inside my vagina – and told me that he didn't see any signs of an infection. What was he expecting, a big, fat, green two-headed monster marching in front of my vagina carrying a sign that said "this way to yeast infection"? As he took off his gloves and washed his hands (???), that voice inside my head got indignant.

"Why are you sittin' there lookin' crazy? Tell him about the itchin' and then tell him to do a pap smear."

I silenced that voice, as well as myself, by deferring to his expertise. After all, he was the gynecologist, not me, so I put my pants back on and stormed out of the examination room, still itching.

By the time I got home, I was fuming. I tried to rationalize what had just happened with the fact that I hadn't known the Dutch words to explain how I was feeling. I congratulated myself for not making a scene and comforted myself with the promise of never going back to that gynecologist. The truth was I'd been afraid to question his authority by insisting on something I knew was necessary. I'd given him authority over my body. Even worse, I hadn't listened to my instinct even though I knew she'd never let me down before. I was disappointed in myself. Still, I went back to my GP and told her about my visit to the gynecologist, at which point she performed the pap test right then and there. The results confirmed a yeast infection, and lucky for me, I was well into my second trimester and was therefore eligible for stronger medication.

A few weeks passed by, and maybe the second round of suppositories had kicked in or perhaps I'd just gotten used to the discomfort south of the border; more likely, complications from the flu I'd caught pushed my itch to the background, where it would remain until I gave birth. On the forefront was a lingering cough. Since that was a normal side effect for me after getting the flu, I didn't think too much of it. But, when I was still coughing three weeks later, I went back to see my GP, asking if she could recommend something stronger than the cough syrup spiked with thyme, which was all that was available over the counter. The cough medicine she prescribed lessened the cough for several days, but a week later I was sitting in her office again, hacking away. I left with a higher dosage of the same cough medicine plus her reason for not prescribing anything stronger.

"You haven't had a fever, Mrs. van Es," she reasoned, "so you haven't really been sick. Since you haven't had a high fever or any other complications, I have no reason to suspect that your baby's in danger by your coughing. I know you still have ten weeks until you deliver, but you're going to have to deal with it."

While I was relieved to hear that my baby was safe, I was appalled that she hadn't suggested any further testing. Did I have bronchitis? Did I have any other virus that only a blood test would catch? I may not have actually been sick, but I wasn't sleeping because the coughing got worse at night. During the day I was so exhausted I didn't even want to play with Chloë let alone schedule appointments with students at the office. The coughing got worse the more I talked. I'd had to leave several students, in the middle of their midterm meetings, to go stand outside in the fresh air.

I'd been coughing around the clock for six weeks and insomnia was taking its toll on my emotional health. My midwife noticed how down I was and advised me to take a week off work. Why hadn't I thought of that? I supposed my American work ethic had been engrained such that not even the more casual Dutch attitude toward work could uproot it. In the Dutch system, family life came first. A forty-hour workweek was the rule rather than the exception. Employees started a new job with at least three full weeks of vacation plus national holidays and could actually use those weeks – all at once – to travel with their families. Sick leave was embedded in the Dutch system: if you were sick, you didn't go to work but you still got paid. Coming from America, where taking too much sick leave was tantamount to blowing your career, I'd never once considered taking off from work. After all, I wasn't *really* sick. On the other hand, spending a week in bed, drinking hot tea and not talking might be just what the doctor ordered, had she ordered it.

My midwife had also suggested I invest in a steamer. I did better than that: a couple times a day I'd retire to the bathroom, turn the shower tap to its highest temperature and inhale the steam. That advice was a godsend, especially at night when my makeshift sauna more than relieved my coughing fits. It actually became a refuge where the water beating against the shower tiles drowned out my cries of frustration and rage at not being able to sleep. One night at around two o'clock in the morning, I was standing in the bathroom steaming, while Chloë and Vinz slept soundly, thinking about my first pregnancy. Back then I couldn't stop singing the praises of the Dutch medical system, which touted strengthening the immune system by letting it fight off infection without the aid of medicine. It was charming that their flu remedy consisted of a high dose of Paracetomol and vitamin C. But it wasn't cute anymore.

About six weeks before my due date, I got hit with another flu bug that ended up in a lung infection. Luckily, I'd gone to my GP before it got serious. Right before prescribing a round of weak antibiotics, she explained that my airways had become hyper-sensitive so that even breathing irritated them, which made me cough. She also explained that my immune system was compromised because of the pregnancy. My body's natural instinct, she explained, was to protect my baby, even at the cost of healing myself. The cough would disappear on its own, she assured me, after I'd given birth. That was all good and well, but when I coughed to the point of vomiting and actually peeing my pants – which I did once in public – I didn't give a damn about her surmising. I wanted that baby out of my body . . . NOW.

My midwife, who'd become more of an advocate, sent me to the hospital with a note that recommended my labor be induced. However, because my condition wasn't life threatening, to me or my baby, the obstetrician wouldn't even consider inducing labor at thirty-six weeks. Or at thirty-seven or even at thirty-eight weeks. I'd fallen into a depression and refused to eat or even get out of bed. My GP suggested I speak with a psychiatrist, especially given the bout of post-partum depression I'd suffered after Chloë's birth. Though I felt it was extreme, I agreed on the off chance that I could somehow get a second recommendation to have my labor induced. The psychiatrist didn't give me that, but she did give me a scare when she suggested, based on my mother's mental illness, that I might be suffering from bipolar disorder. "Bipolar disorder?" I thought to myself before telling her exactly why I was feeling depressed: I'd been coughing around the clock for nearly ten weeks, and I was exhausted. There was no guarantee the baby would be born on time, and the thought of six weeks in my condition depressed me even more. I wanted the baby out and my body back.

I was thirty-nine weeks pregnant when my obstetrician finally agreed to induce my labor. I coughed through three hours of contractions until finally, on May 25, 2007, Paige Antonia was born. After the maelstrom of emotions that I'd suffered during my pregnancy, I was grateful for the calm following Paige's birth. Within a couple of days, my coughing stopped completely and my yeast infection cleared up. Although my GP had been right about my pregnant body not being capable of healing my lungs and nurturing a baby, I'd lost confidence in her. In principle I agreed with minimizing medical intervention for such a natural process, but when I'd felt that distressed, I wish she'd been proactive with her treatments. We decided to let her go.

Because of my late-term depression, the psychiatrist I'd spoken to recommended we continue our appointments, at least until after the first six weeks, which, according to her, could be the most detrimental to my emotional stability. I felt relieved to have professional support. She explained that postpartum depression was not inevitable. Sure, fluctuating hormone levels shortly after birth, which contributed to depression, were normal, but I could certainly influence their impact by making better choices. She urged me to take a nap whenever Paige slept.

"There is a link between not getting enough sleep and depression," she informed me. Since I was nursing Paige twice in the middle of the night, napping was imperative.

"Your house does not have to be spotless," she said. "Yes, wash the dishes; yes, clean the toilets; yes, do the laundry. But, you don't have to cook gourmet meals; you don't have to scrub the floors; and you don't have to iron, fold and put away the clothes. Do only the minimum of housekeeping."

I took the bassinette out of our bedroom and found myself sleeping more soundly. Vinz agreed to cook a few times a week but drew a line at housework. I took him up on his offer to hire a housekeeper to come in once a week to vacuum and mop the floors. Chloë had already started school, so I had the entire morning to take hours-long walks while Paige slept in her stroller to keep up my contact with people. By the end of the sixth week, which is when the risk of postpartum depression is at the highest, I was emotionally fit. Paige was sleeping through the night, I was rested and feeling optimistic about my expanded family. I felt calm.

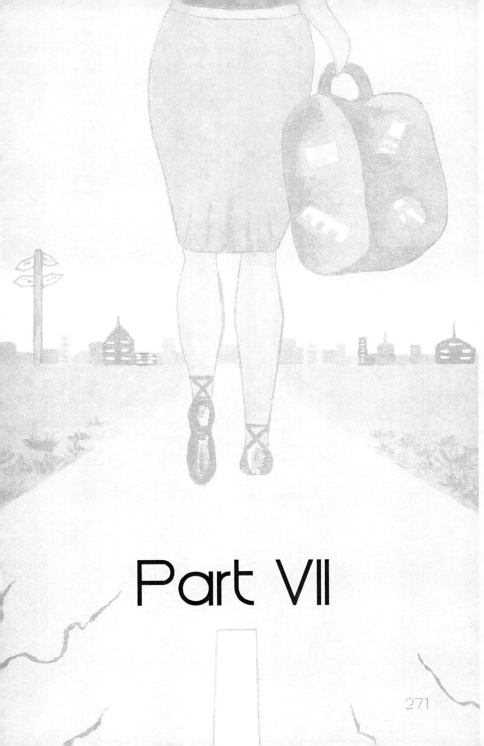

Part VII

Whenever I watched Chloë holding and kissing her baby sister, who was almost four years younger, I couldn't help thinking about my relationship with Felicia, who was four years older than me. Chloë showered Paige with affection; obviously, she adored her baby sister. Had Felicia ever felt that way about me? Whenever Chloë held Paige in her lap or kissed her little hands and cheeks, I prayed for a closeness between them that my sister and I were never blessed to feel.

Being from my mother's first marriage, Felicia favored her father as much as I favored mine. She had light skin and thick black hair while my skin was caramel-colored and my hair was light brown. She was always heavy set while I'd been dubbed "skinny-minny" by my father and "French fry" by the neighborhood kids. I learned best from books and school; she learned by taking things apart and figuring out for herself how to put them back together.

Surviving our childhood was probably the only other thing we'd ever had in common, and we didn't even experience its aftermath in the same way. Felicia had never asked to take over the household when Cory died. At fourteen, she was thrust into the role of caretaker because my mother couldn't cope. Felicia went to the store, cooked and cleaned for Dawn and me. She must have felt responsible for our welfare when an adult should have been taking care of her. Being the oldest, she witnessed things that I, the youngest, didn't even remember, like seeing my mother at Cory's deathbed. I hadn't even been at the hospital the night Dawn died. Felicia had been, and she was the voice I heard saying, "Carolyn, wake up. Dawn didn't make it."

According to Felicia I became the favorite; according to me it was, as usual, Cory and Dawn, dead but at the center of my mother's everything. She'd repeatedly committed the cardinal sin of parenting: comparing children. Unfortunately, Felicia always came out wanting, and that caused friction between us. She praised me because I caused very little trouble. Up until I graduated, I'd come home after school and do my homework. I got good grades and got a part-time job, at which I earned my own lunch money. I rarely went to parties on the weekend. My only sources of entertainment were the pom pon squad and flag corps and the track team.

Felicia, on the other hand, seemed to aggravate my mother. To show off her love of music, Felicia would blast the latest Parliament/Funkadelic album forgetting to watch the clock in her enthusiasm. My mother would come home from work, immediately turn off the record player and proceed to fuss at Felicia about her bump-de-bump music.

My mother isolated my sisters and me from her extended family. She'd resented her aunts and uncles for their alleged mistreatment of Grandma Thelma, who, according to my mother, was the most beautiful of the three girls and most vivacious of all her five brothers and sisters put together. My mother hated their insistence that children should be seen and not heard. She'd kept us away from them to protect our fragile confidence from being crushed under their domineering and condescending ideas of how to deal with children. For most of our childhood, she'd been pissed at what she'd perceived as betrayal whenever

Felicia sought out the company of her family.

Perhaps Felicia's most unforgivable trespass was her constant association with our mother's baby brother, the one who was there when my brother was stabbed. She'd been in high school when her brother and one of her cousins bought a fish market around the corner from where my mother had grown up. Back in her day, it had been a thriving community. By the time the fish market opened its doors, it had become a slum, replete with drugs, thugs and other unmentionable elements. Unfortunately, that environment had rubbed off on Felicia, who initiated a relationship with alcohol from which she would find it almost impossible to disassociate herself.

Nor did my mother approve of Felicia's friends. She'd always hung around with an older crowd, and the older she got, the older her friends became. My mother had accused my sister of running around with low-class people who never gave a damn about her. She'd heard that this girl had been a prostitute and that girl had been on drugs. None of the girls Felicia ran around with had had an education. My mother had sacrificed so much to raise us in a safe environment and lectured us on the importance of not getting pregnant and making something of ourselves, and my sister must have broken her heart by doing exactly the opposite of what she'd taught us.

Ever since I could remember, my mother had hammered education into our heads. Since my sister's was apparently as hard as a rock, my mother had to invest in jackhammer tactics over the years, which may have been borderline abusive. Felicia was never interested in school, so when the truant officer came knocking on the door she would be subjected to my mother's rants about how she wouldn't amount to anything if she didn't go to school.

Ironically, my mother had hated school as much as my sister did. How many times had she headed off to school only to hide herself in some bushes half the day so Grandma Thelma wouldn't suspect her of playing hooky? My mother had been just as hardheaded as she'd accused Felicia of being. How many times had I listened to my mother chastise herself for not listening to my grandmother? Unfortunately, she seemed to forget those stories when she mercilessly jacked up my sister for not wanting to "better herself".

Our traumatic childhood was made worse by the fact that a piece of my mother had stopped living when those kids died. She showed Felicia and me very little affection, probably because becoming too attached to us wasn't a risk she was willing to take. She'd showed very little warmth despite doing her best to keep us with her. So when she wasn't working the secretarial job she abhorred, she was sleeping. Felicia, in turn, drank for her comfort. They both tuned out, each in her own way.

By the time I left college, my longing to feel close to Felicia had changed. I'd felt sorry for her. My mother and I had known for years that Felicia drank but had been reluctant to label her an alcoholic, not even after she'd been fired from job after job and been evicted from apartment after apartment. When, at twenty-five, I'd moved to D.C., my mother would tell me about every misstep my sister took that led her back to "stay" with my mother in her one-bedroom apartment. Every time I called or went back home to visit, I felt like I hadn't moved a mile. That pity at her lifestyle had been gradually changing into anger for putting so much stress on my mother's back. Hadn't my mother been through enough without having to deal with the drama that my sister's drinking created?

Whenever Felicia got beat up, she'd run straight to my mother. At any time of day or night, when she was drunk and cantankerous, she'd bang on my mother's door demanding to be let in. When she lost a job, she'd go to my mother for money, food and shelter. I was starting to hate my sister for upsetting my mother's already fragile mental stability. I was hating her for ruining my chances to have a close relationship with a sibling. I hated her for wrecking her life when our brother and sister had had theirs taken away too soon.

By the time I'd moved to New Orleans, I'd become ashamed of the dysfunctional dance my mother and sister were performing together. My sister would gather up a few weeks' worth of misfortune and lay them at my mother's front door. And my mother would open that front door as wide as the hinges would allow and invite them all in, not because of any illusions that it would heal my sister but because she was afraid of losing her. I'd told Vinz a bit about the situation but mostly kept it to myself. I wasn't sure he'd understand why I felt responsible that Felicia had been dealt such a shitty hand in life. He certainly wouldn't understand why I'd sink into a depression of my own every time my mother gave me details about my sister's lifestyle. So, when he'd asked me to move away with him, I'd been reluctant to add that issue to the list of reasons I couldn't accept his offer. I didn't want to put that burden on him. I didn't want him to think that I was like them. I wanted him to see me for myself.

I didn't tell my mother for a couple of weeks that I'd decided to move to Holland. I'd been afraid she'd suffer another nervous breakdown. I'd felt guilty at the thought of leaving her alone to deal with my sister's drinking problem. I'd felt even guiltier about my relief at the thought of leaving them alone to figure out their relationship. When I'd finally told her, she'd seemed happy enough for me and assured me that there wasn't anything in America for me. Deep down I believed that putting an ocean between us, I could somehow remove myself from the middle of the dysfunction.

Eight years, two children and one continent later, I was still in the middle of their drama. One afternoon a few months after Paige had been born, my mother called me, in tears.

"I just can't take it any more," my mother sobbed. "I didn't have anybody else to call. I don't know what to do. I'm so sick of this mess."

Once I found out she wasn't in any danger or in need of an ambulance, I asked if I could call her right back. She'd called exactly twenty minutes before I had to pick Chloë up from school, so I had to quickly arrange for a neighbor to bring her home. That done, I called my mother back.

"Felicia woke me up at two o'clock in the morning banging on my bedroom window. I wasn't gonna let her in but I saw her face. Oh Carolyn, it was black and blue and all swollen up. I let her in and she looked like she'd been hit by a car. She was fighting with that girl again. When I told her I didn't want to hear anymore, she threatened to knock me in the head. I called the police on her and told them to take her back to jail."

I was in tears myself at the precise moment, of course, that my neighbor rang the doorbell to drop Chloë off. I didn't even try to hide my tears and thanked my neighbor for her help. Chloë started crying. I sat down on the couch with her and cuddled her as best I could while listening to my mother sobbing on the other line. Luckily Paige was still sleeping.

"Has Felicia ever hit you, Mom?" I asked, not really wanting to know the answer.

"No, she's never hit me. But she's threatened me before. I know it's that damn drinking, but this has got to stop."

"Are you willing to take out a restraining order against her?"

"I guess so," she responded.

I spent the next hour calling the Indianapolis Police Department, the courts, my mother's social worker and my mother, trying to arrange this restraining order. Once I hung up the phone, assured that my mother was calm, I let Chloë comfort me with her child's hugs and kisses me and ask me why I'd been crying.

"Because Aunty Fee Fee's been bad."

"What did Aunty Fee Fee do, Mama?" Chloë pushed.

"She said some mean things to Grandma."

"What did she say?"

"That doesn't really matter, baby," I explained gently. "She was really naughty and made Grandma cry."

"Does she have to take a time-out in the hallway?" she asked naively.

"Yes, baby. She has to go to the hallway," I replied, wishing it were that easy.

My guilt for surviving the past and building a healthy, functional, happy life for myself and my family kept pulling me back into the middle of more than twenty years of drinking and suicide attempts and depressions and tears and anger. A few days after that latest episode, I felt drained. I was sick of feeling guilty because my father had claimed me when Felicia's had disappeared from her young life. I was tired of feeling guilty because my mother and father had always believed in me. Not only that, but there had been a slew of teachers who'd seen my talent for learning and for languages and had opened door after door for me. I couldn't help but wonder how different Felicia's life would have been had someone, just one person, believed in her, too. I was damn sick and tired of feeling that I didn't deserve happiness when my family – my mother and sister, that is – were so miserable.

It had to stop, and I was the only one who could put a stop to it. I eventually explained to my mother that I no longer wanted to hear about my sister's escapades after she'd been drinking. I explained that I was no longer willing to put myself in the middle of their relationship. Whenever my mother started talking about my sister's problems or their fights, I would politely tell her I had to hang up and see to my kids. I eventually forgave my sister for the money she'd taken from me, the lies she'd told and for the betrayals against my mother and me. I accepted the reality that

Felicia and I might never be close. Although I didn't agree with what she was doing to herself, I accepted that her lifestyle was her choice. I didn't know where she'd been, so who was I to judge where she was now? Most significantly, I let myself off the hook. I forgave myself for surviving. I reminded myself that I was worthy of the happiness I'd generated. I gave myself permission to continue to shape my life around the new identity I was forging that would focus on where my life was going rather than on the tragedies of my childhood.

*F*or years I'd wanted to build up a home-based career; alas, I'd never advanced beyond daydreaming about sleeping in and doing conference calls in my pajamas. I had no idea what I could do or what I had to offer. I'd already considered manufacturing cross-stitch patterns, as needlework had long been a hobby. I'd also gotten enthusiastic about designing a line of children's clothing. I'd gotten as far as naming my label: "mama's girl" and visualizing top quality t-shirts with catchy texts such as "give me a break; I'm two". However, I couldn't imagine myself spending eight hours a day, five days a week doing either hobby as a career. Paige was already three months, and I only had three months before the end of my maternity leave. I knew I wasn't going back to the university, and if I wanted to work from home, I'd better find my vocation. And quick.

The timing must have been right and the universe must have been answering my silent prayers to help me find my passion when, Ineke, a former professor from the University of Maryland called that she was in Holland and would like to see me. I hadn't seen her since she'd left the US to return to Berlin where her husband, a Liechtensteiner, was a professor of science. This Dutch woman giving a course on Puerto Rican literature had intrigued me from day one. I always had the impression that, as a scholar, she'd taught on the fringe because of her focus on the African influence on Latin American culture. Before taking her course, I'd never known there were black people in Latin America. After that course, I learned that black Americans and black Latinos actually had a similar socio-cultural history that could do more to unite our experience than what nationality and language did to distance it. That Dutch woman was also the first professor who, during my graduate studies, saw and encouraged my potential as a scholar. Like Señorita Wagner, she opened up a whole new world to me.

I was thrilled to meet and catch up with her, and when I did, she informed me about her current project, which dealt with the Dutch colonizing presence in the New World. Her analyses gave prominence to the Creole voices using their vernacular to articulate their own post-colonial identity politics. Although English was among the five languages she spoke fluently, she was concerned about writing a book in it. I offered to proofread her finished manuscript. She accepted, and once again we were working together.

Once again, Ineke had inspired me, and in my own way, I wanted to give something back. She may not have been a tenured professor anymore at a respectable university, but she'd given rein to her expertise and her passion to conduct research as an independent scholar in an area of study where few others dared to tread. I hadn't managed to earn a Ph.D. But I learned that I had developed a set of skills in graduate school that I could use now. I could conduct research, read in foreign languages, think critically about all that I read and write at a high level. When our project was done, I'd already decided to present myself as a freelance copy editor, translator and writer.

But first I had to get through Vinz, the consummate businessman.

"Let me see your business plan," he said, holding his hand out.

"I don't need one. I'm working from home; I'm not borrowing money from the bank."

"Where are you going to get your clients? How do you know there's a market for a freelance editor, translator and writer? What are you doing to advertise?" He pelted the questions like he was shooting a BB gun.

Once I got over feeling attacked and defensive about my lack of preparation, I started looking at a business plan as a to-do list, which made the process less intimidating. Vinz outlined the SWOT model for me, and as I spent the following weeks considering my strengths, weaknesses, opportunities and threats, I started feeling empowered. I saw the potential and acknowledged the fact that I had the experience and skills to be successful. We sat down together and looked at how losing my income would affect us. Luckily, we'd made some lifestyle choices that allowed me to leave my job. We had no credit card debt, Vinz drove a company car and I'd bought an old car from his aunt after years of using public transportation. The mortgage on our house had been based solely on his salary, so even though that had meant a smaller, less luxurious house, we would always be able to pay our mortgage. Put simply, our decision years ago to live within our means gave me the chance now to pursue my dream of working from home.

The next step was to answer his question: how did I plan to succeed providing freelance word services? After being stumped for a couple weeks, I finally came up with an answer: by establishing a balance that would allow me time for my family, the time to deliver a quality product on deadline as well as time for myself. How would I accomplish that though? Discipline. During the sixteen hours per week when Chloë was at school and Paige at daycare, I would put my butt in my chair and work. I would make choices that supported my goal, so even though the breakfast dishes lay stacked on the kitchen counter, I would put my butt in a chair and work. If a friend invited me for coffee, I would put my butt in a chair and work.

To be successful I had to minimize my stress levels. I knew I didn't work well under pressure, so to avoid impossible deadlines, I decided to take on no more than two long-term projects at a time. Instead of spending on advertising, I would slowly build a reputation of excellence and expertise that would be spread word of mouth. Sure enough, during my first year as a freelancer, I was commissioned to translate *De deseurters*, a novel by critically-acclaimed Curaçaoan, Frank Martinus Arion.

It took me the better part of that first year to translate it but I did so alongside writing advertorials for an English-language newspaper with a respectable circulation among the Dutch expatriate community. Those two long-term assignments were precisely what I needed to build my confidence, establish myself as a freelancer as well as create a network. They also helped me to admit that my true passion was the writing side of my business. I wanted to write an original, creative text. I wanted to write a book, a memoir. I longed to put a voice behind the experiences that had led me to where I was and the person I'd become, but hadn't dared voice that desire to Vinz. Nor to myself. Most authors couldn't make a living from their writing alone. What made me think I'd succeed where countless others had failed?

Besides, who would be interested in reading about my life even if I could spike it with a positive message? Dreaming about inspiring black women to travel, as a tool to transcend the limitations of their identity was little more than my indulgence in self-importance. Who did I think I was anyway?

"Well, that woman went and wrote Eat, Pray and Love. You could do the same thing for black women," suggested my voice.

Indeed, I could.

There were three factors that were instrumental in spurring me on to write this memoir. The first was reading *The Artist's Way*. When I'd first heard about Julia Cameron's seminal book on breaking through writer's block, I had no clue that the self-defeating thoughts I'd been having were normal. The gist of the book is that most burgeoning writers are confronted with their fears, which manifests as the inability to put word to page. It's also quite normal to listen to the self-sabotaging justifications our fears place foremost in our minds as soon as we resolve to tap into our creative reserves. What Cameron's book offers are tools to deal with writer's block, which never disappears. The trick is to write through it, which is what I learned to do.

Before I even considered writing my memoir, I'd committed to the morning pages exercise recommended by Cameron. For months, I'd wake up at 6:00 am and while my family slept, I'd spend thirty minutes writing through the thoughts that were loitering about in my mind. At first, this freestyle writing exercise was excruciating, so I was reduced to spending the first ten minutes writing about how stupid it was. In as little as a few weeks, I'd already moved past this stage and wandered onto the next act, which was to find the courage to write through all the negative thoughts and judgments I'd had about myself, other people, the world at large. My heart would race as I wrote about the resentment I'd harbored toward Vinz because his life, not to mention his body, seemed not to change after we'd had our children. How did I dare feel this way when he'd been so good to me? Nevertheless, I wrote about it, and by the end of the thirty minutes, I felt free. I'd found a safe release for my emotions and thoughts.

After months of repeating this process, I actually became comfortable being honest with myself and my feelings. By committing to these morning pages, I'd also developed discipline. So, when I didn't know where to begin to write my memoir, I decided to follow the same process. I'd sit for thirty minutes a day and just write about my life. As with the morning pages, my only rule with writing was to leave judgment outside, so whatever memories surfaced, no matter how painful or how trite, I'd write them down. A few weeks later, I was already able to see a few patterns, and from that point, when I sat down for my thirty-minute memoir sessions, I'd write freestyle about high school or living in D.C. or my lovers or anger toward my mother. By the sixth month, I'd exhausted my memory deck. Coupled with the morning pages, I was feeling free and light. I could actually admit that I had a way with words.

Sarah, a friend of mine who'd just moved to Amsterdam from D.C., suggested I start a blog. At the time I had no clue what a blog was, much less how it could improve my writing skills. Sarah traveled the world for her work in development and had landed in some of the most volatile places. She'd used blogging to keep her friends and family updated, but also, I suspected, as a tool to download some of the horrors she'd witnessed. She'd explained that blogging had helped her progress from journaling to writing for an audience. The feedback she received in the form of readers' comments had sustained her.

It was enough to convince me to start a blog of my own. My plan was to post pieces about my experiences as a black woman living and traveling abroad. As I wanted to reach out to black women in particular and inspire them to travel, I wanted to paint a true picture of a day in the life of a black expatriate. I loved it and posted often. I built up a modest community of readers as well as creating my own online network of other expatriate women of all races and nationalities. My blog even won the Jury's Vote at the 2009 Black Weblogs Prize.

All the while I was continuing with my morning pages. So, when a friend forwarded me some information about a workshop held in Amsterdam in English on the art of writing memoir, I jumped on it. Rebecca Walker would be facilitating it. I had no idea who she was, so I Googled her to make sure she'd actually written a memoir before forking over seventy-five euros for a three-hour workshop. Her first memoir, *Black, White and Jewish,* recounted the anguish she'd suffered traveling from the scant, lonely world of her famous mother, Alice Walker, to a posh, yet equally lonely life with her Jewish father, the famous civil rights lawyer, Mel Levanthal. I couldn't believe my luck. I'd actually be meeting someone else who'd also grown up with shifting identities.

I wasn't sure what to expect from the workshop since I'd participated in very few. It was pleasantly surprising that Ms. Walker didn't even mention her famous parents, nor did she take up time boosting her own ego. Instead, she began by asking each of us five participants about our individual projects. Each of us had not only the time, but also the space in which to elaborate on where we were in the process and what our goals were for writing a memoir. She had the ability to focus her attention, undivided, on our projects and give us feedback, suggestions and encouragement to keep writing as none of us was very far along in the process.

I had come to a crossroads of sorts. I'd finished my brainstorming; I'd written down every detail of every memory that dared poke its head inside mine. The contents of my memoirs were there, but I didn't quite know where to proceed from there. While I was sharing the background of my project, I started crying. She, and the other participants, empathized with the emotional impact of this type of writing. Instead of advising me on my next step, Ms. Walker went a step further: she validated my desire to write a book with a message. I'd never shared my writing process with a professional memoirist who'd experienced firsthand the contradictory events and emotions that I was writing about. While we ended up doing only a few writing exercises, it was Ms. Walker's insights about my project that inspired me to continue writing.

The third factor that inspired me to write had been sitting next to me at Ms. Walker's workshop. When I'd entered the room, I couldn't help but notice the beautiful, ageless black woman already comfortable in her seat, her notebook open and her pen placed on top of it. With a smile that was as sincere as it was warm, she'd beckoned me to sit next to her.

"Hello. My name is Lois," she introduced herself.

After I told her my name, I listened while she explained that she'd signed up for the workshop as a tool to help her collect and organize the events in her colorful life. She wasn't writing a memoir; rather, she sought to apply the techniques to produce a documentary. When it was her turn to speak about her project, she talked about her desegregating a university as well as serving as the first African-American President of the National Christian Students Union. Her sister, Thelma Mothershed, had been one of the Little Rock Nine, the young high school students who tried to integrate Central High School in Little Rock against the orders of Governor Orval Faubus. Lois remembered what happened to her sister as well as to her father, who was in the segregated US Army from the Battle of the Bulge to Okinawa, and she wanted to leave those memories as a legacy for her own children.

I felt an instant kinship with this woman with the short afro and strong cheekbones. In her day black women simply did not travel abroad. Yet she did, and in the meantime, she met a Dutchman whom she married and followed back to Holland. They've been married for nearly fifty years. She was a pioneer herself, yet in a less historical way. At the end of the workshop, as we were putting on our coats, she handed me a business card.

"If you're interested, I'd like to invite you to a group I belong to called Sister Sista. We're black women from around the world who meet the first Saturday of every month to talk, laugh and eat. I think you'd enjoy meeting other sisters here in Holland."

A few months later I walked through the doors of sisterhood. I sat on the couch and looked around the hostess's living room. There were about twenty soul sisters from around the world. I heard Spanish being spoken, Dutch, Papiamento, English. A Kenyan woman was returning to her country, that being her last gathering. A light-skinned beauty, with crazy curls, was born and raised in Curaçao but spent her adult life in Holland. She was in the final stages of her dissertation. A woman from the Dominican Republic who grew up in Florida spoke Spanish to me. Lois, the walking history book, was there.

Our hostess, another wise, ageless Curaçaoan woman who'd married a Dutchman, asked me if I wanted some *bol*.

"Well, sure," I stammered. "Only, I'm not sure what it is." Then a couple other sisters joined her as she explained that it was more or less a fruit salad – with a bit of white wine and sweet liqueur.

"But at each party in Curaçao there is served *bol*. Try it."

I sat there eating my fruit, listening to the chaotic discussions and sudden bursts of laughter taking place all over the room. It seemed like every one was talking at the same time. I'd come home. I hadn't had this feeling since I stepped off the plane in Cuba. I had been lonely, and desperately wanting a girlfriend. I didn't realize how I'd longed for that connection with someone who could understand my experience without my having to explain myself. It was the only part of my life at that point that had been sorely neglected.

On the surface the only thing I had in common with this group of women who would become my soul sisters was that we identified ourselves as being black. The more gatherings I attended, though, the more I recognized that the connection went deeper. Rebecca Cole, who had left the US to be with her Dutch boyfriend, had founded the group seven years previously. After they split up, she decided to stay.

Although she'd made connections with white Dutch and expatriate women, she'd told me how desperate she'd been to talk about something as mundane as where she could get her hair done. She'd posted a message on a forum on Expatica.com asking if there were other black women in Holland and had been thrilled with six or seven positive responses. That small group evolved into the seventy or so members we are today.

Rebecca was adamant that the group remain free of political agendas. There are no membership fees, guest lists or roll calls. There is no calendar of events save one monthly gathering where we laugh out loud about a particular celebrity's latest gaffe or share our respective experiences as black women in the world. Sister Sista represents the ultimate integration and reconnection. I've rebuilt a system of support and friendship even though we all have different nationalities – Nigerian, English, Curacaoan, Columbian, Trinidadian, American. Many of us are married to Dutch men and have interracial children, so we're a solid support system for each other to talk about the particular issues that come up because of our situation.

Through the group I met an interesting woman early in the process of writing this book. Jhosan grew up in Trinidad before moving to New York for her bachelor's and master's degrees. We met one afternoon in her apartment, which she and her husband, also from Trinidad, had just bought. The walls in her hallway were streaked with paint ranging from orange to burnt umber. She'd been decorating as a way to fill her time while she looked for a job.

I asked her what her impression of black Americans had been before she'd moved to the US. She explained that the image that most Trinidadians had was formed by television and movies. She'd grown up watching *Beat Street* and other movies portraying blacks as having to struggle. She elaborated:

"Today you have socially responsible people who have movies that show black people in a positive light, but back then they always portrayed black people struggling in the ghetto, even in the positive movies, with the mother or single parent making sacrifices so the children could have the best. But they always had to struggle. That was the message."

Other Trinidadians who'd returned after a stint in the States had confirmed that message. But Jhosan had been quick to add that those perspectives may have been skewed.

"People from the islands tend to go and settle in one community in Flatbush in Brooklyn or in the West Indian community in Atlanta. A lot of them are illegal immigrants and have to struggle, so you got the impression that things would be very, very difficult and that white people would always try to suppress you because of your color. The mindset was that things would be harder for people like you who were that shade of brown."

What set Jhosan apart was her own mindset. She'd become convinced that limiting oneself by limiting one's mind is what gets us all into trouble. When she began to "live outside of her own mind" the world opened up to her. She explained that in Trinidad blacks live alongside whites, and Muslims alongside Hindus. She recalled her Muslim neighbors helping her family put up Christmas decorations. The bank where she worked advocated all employees dressing up in native gear to celebrate the various ethnic holidays. Her background served as a springboard to deal with people on an individual level.

I asked her how living in America and then Holland changed her, and she replied that the experiences have taught her to think wider and to reject putting limitations on her thoughts and aspirations.

"If I want to do something, I go out and I do it. I don't think that I can't do it because I don't have the ability. If I can't do it it's because I'm too lazy or I'm not making the time for it."

"In Trinidad," she continued, "I didn't know what I didn't know. That was my world, and the other countries were on a map or in an atlas. I could not have perceived of living in Europe or in the US because I had no imagination of what that would be. So the experience of living abroad has shown me that the world is really small, and that people are just people."

And with that, Jhosan validated my reason for needing to write this memoir. I didn't know what I didn't know and I didn't know that my identity, how I saw myself, was dynamic until I started traveling outside my comfort zone. My travels literally drove me all over the United States before flying me down to Mexico and the Caribbean and then across the ocean to Europe. I've become acquainted with nearly one hundred cities in seventeen countries spread over three continents, each of which, through a slight gesture or a grandiose revelation, gave me insight into the various identities that have been residing deep inside my consciousness, safe from the harshness of my life.

Through my physical and metaphysical travels through the limitations imposed by my prefabricated identity, I've learned that I have the power to determine the course of my own life. As with any traveling, I was bound to stumble upon a crossroad or two in order to get to where I was going. To be sure, many of those crossroads seemed to pop up at the most inconvenient spots in my life, making it hard to make those crucial decisions. Should I move to Holland and marry this man or should I hightail it back home where I felt secure in the safety of familiar expectations? Should I let fear hold me to a career path that immobilized me or should I trust my instinct and pursue a passion that would free up time and emotional space to be there for my family?

At forty I gave birth to a new identity that was no longer shrouded in the tragedies of my childhood. I was no longer the girl who resented the world yet expected pity from it because her brother and sister died when she was still too young to even contemplate what it meant to be alive. I recast the shame I felt as a young adult about her mentally ill mother living on disability into admiration for a woman who had such a tremendous faith in my life that she believed in my future even when I didn't. I tempered my rage toward a community that tried to silence my existence and a culture that tried to nullify it, and made space to forgive, not just those institutions but myself for having bought into their standards.

Three years into my forties I welcome every opportunity to look at myself in the mirror of two families who support, embrace and love me for who I am. I look into the fair faces of my lovely daughters and see who I've become. They are a reflection of a woman who respects and accepts her own body. I no longer battle my hair; I let it do its thing. I keep it well groomed, not by spending two hours a week and hundreds of euros a month going to the beauty shop. My hair is healthy because I'm healthy. I get regular facials and have my mustache and armpits waxed, though not out of vanity. My daughters are a reflection of a woman who takes pride in her appearance because *ze zit gewoon lekker in haar vel*, a Dutch expression which I take to mean that I feel at ease with myself from the inside and that manifests to my exterior. My kids are a reflection of a woman who has become confident in the wisdom that she has an inner power.

I shouldn't be here.

That's what many will say.

After all, I was a poor black girl from a broken home and a broken community. I should have ended up addicted, on welfare and with at least one baby daddy. No, I shouldn't be sitting here in the Dutch lap of luxury writing this brutally honest memoir about my relationship with my black female body and how living and traveling abroad and marriage to a white Dutchman have transformed that relationship.

But here I am doing what few others have managed.

I'm a black woman abroad, and I shouldn't be here.

But I am.

Left to right: Baby Paige, me, Chloe, Vinz
Netherlands, 2008

CPSIA information can be obtained at www.ICGtesting.com
Printed in the USA
LVOW082305020512

280032LV00003B/70/P